Finding the Treasures Left Along the Trail

~

My Cherokee Heritage

Iris E. Stout

A Note From the Author

The research and writing of this book was a shared effort with my husband, Brian. His interest in the Native American culture was expanded and intensified by this project. We spent many hours reading and discussing the volumes of information and unique stories that we were able to locate in a variety of resources, including legal documents.

Acknowledgements

We thank the individuals who have contributed so much historical information which allowed us to complete this book.

Dedication

This book is dedicated to my family, particularly our two sons and four grandchildren.

It is also in memory of my parents, Mr. and Mrs. O. M. Story, who never had the opportunity to know the detailed Cherokee heritage of my Grandmother, Minerva Courtney Story.

Table of Contents

Author Biography

Iris E. Stout was born in Oklahoma and spent her elementary and intermediate school years in southern Missouri. Her Dad's job took the family to the Upper Peninsula of Michigan where she completed high school and first met her future husband, Brian. She attended college and became certified as a laboratory and x-ray technician, and later became certified as an audio-metric technician.

After marriage, she and Brian pursued his career with the U. S. Department of Agriculture, Forest Service, and raised two sons. The numerous moves the family made still resulted in several interesting jobs in the medical field and positions in the court system. Her strong support allowed the family to flourish, even with fifteen moves throughout the United States in 34 years.

During their last assignment as Forest Supervisor in Wyoming, she was vital in maintaining close relationships among Forest staff and assisted the Bridger-Teton National Forest with specially designed .public participation programs such as wilderness horse packing trips. She and her Morgan horse, "Beauty", experienced some incredible adventures into several Wyoming wilderness areas. These trips proved invaluable in opening communications with a wide variety of groups and individuals.

Their two sons went on to become a dentist and an engineer, and have their own successful businesses today.

Iris became a member of the Cherokee Nation in 1995, which intensified her desire to learn more about her Native American heritage. "Finding the Treasures Left Along the Trail" has been exciting, and learning of the numerous important individuals that contributed so much to early American history has been incredible!

"Finding the Treasures Left Along the Trail – My Cherokee Heritage" presents a historical account of significant contributions made by a family with roots in Europe and in the Cherokee Nation here in America. The book discloses information seldom taught in American history classes in our public schools, and sheds a very different view of the Native American society and its major influence on settlement and development of the United States of America. Even our egalitarian democracy came from the Native American (Iroquois) form of government.

You will read stories of family members educated as attorneys, a member raised to the rank of General in the Civil War, and numerous individuals elected to lead the Nation as Principal Chiefs.

The Carpenters from Devonshire, England, first arrived on the North American Continent in 1627, and the incredible journey begins!

A Search for My Cherokee Heritage

Chapter 1 – The Journey

From my early childhood, I was made aware that my paternal Grandmother Story was part Cherokee. I never had the privilege of knowing her, as she died in 1920, nineteen years before I was born. Details of her Cherokee heritage were unknown or seldom discussed within the family. Her death was the result of the worldwide flu pandemic that occurred between 1918 and 1920. Records indicate 500 million people were infected worldwide and 50 to 100 million died.

Grandmother Minerva Story (front) and sister Jessye

Dad was only three years old at the time, when he and his two sisters went to live for a few years with their maternal grandparents, John and Ann Courtney. This is probably the main reason so little information was passed down about the Native American heritage of their mother.

One story I can remember being told by the family was that Grandpa Story's family did not approve of his marriage to Minerva Courtney because of her Indian background.

When the Story family moved on to California, Grandpa Story decided to remain in Oklahoma to raise his three young children. I can also remember my dad, in his later years, would tell the medical technicians when they drew blood for tests, "You can take the white blood, but leave the Cherokee blood alone." Dad, obviously, inherited a degree of pride in his mother's background.

For much of my life, I knew very little of the Native American culture or my Cherokee heritage. Because my Grandmother Story was registered on the Dawes Roll in 1909, I was able to register as a citizen of the Cherokee Nation in 1995.

My interest intensified in my Native American background after becoming a member of the Cherokee Nation.

In 2009, I found a letter in Mom's Bible from a distant cousin of mine, who provided limited information on the ancestry of Dad's mother. It included one Native American name which turned out to be Cherokee. I decided to see if any information could be found on the internet, about I-NO-WA-GA-GO-LO-NU-GI, born in 1790.

Finding this name led me to "Family-Tree-Maker.com, Cherokee Genealogy", where I discovered much information on my ancestors. ᴵ

Realizing I was now one of the oldest members of the family, I needed to record the genealogical information before it was lost. After 5 years of research, it was evident this was more than just a family genealogy report. It also became clear that there were many discrepancies in the variety of documents, stories, and reports that were available. Putting the pieces of the puzzle together was an interesting and challenging process which I hope might help others with their search for family history. This research effort was a joint effort with my husband.

Finding the many stories of my lineage has been exciting and beyond belief! The discovery of a letter from Benjamin Franklin and the important individuals that contributed so much to Cherokee history, and early American history, was more than I could have imagined.

As I began my search, my husband was looking for a way to express his concerns about the declining conditions of our human environment, forestry in particular. After 34 years as a professional forester, he was convinced there was something missing in the management principles being applied to our remaining forests. Could the missing link be the ability to observe and understand the complexity and details of nature?

Other cultures, such as the Native Americans, seem to have a much more in-depth appreciation for our connectedness and dependency on our surroundings for survival. Research for his book, "Trees of Life - Our Forests in Peril" (find and purchase at: http://tinyurl.com/p9n9obe) published in 2013, created a joint opportunity to reach beyond a genealogical search and to develop an understanding and appreciation for the Native American culture and wisdom they developed over thousands of years of empirical observations of nature.

By piecing together information from many sources, I was able to trace my Native American lineage from the current time back to Thomas Pasmere Carpenter, who arrived on the North American Continent from Devonshire, England in 1627. He was born in 1607 to Robert Carpenter and Susan Pasmere Jeffery. The Carpenter family lineage was from nobility, with Robert being the son of William Carpenter III and Anne Stroud.

Reviewing early European history allowed me to trace the Carpenter family's ancestry back as far as King Charlemagne and the Middle Ages. Research also revealed stories of several individuals that contributed significantly to early Cherokee and American history. My heritage would be incomplete without the inclusion of these important stories.

I was amazed to find so much information on the Carpenter family's European history. Thomas Pasmere Carpenter was descended from the noble Anglo-Norman family of Viscomte Gullaume de Melun le Carpentier. Gullaume de Melun was known as "William the Carpenter", and was a French nobleman who participated in the Reconquista in Spain and in the First Crusade. He was known for his strength in battle, whence he earned his nickname, "The Carpenter".

The First Crusade occurred from 1096 to 1099, and was the attempt to retake the Holy Lands taken by the Muslim Conquests during 632-661. In 711, the Muslims conquered the Ibertan Peninsula. The Reconquista of Spain ended in 1492, when the Christian army drove the Muslims from Granada. In 1502, the Spanish Crown ordered all Muslims forcibly converted to Christianity.

According to twelfth-century monk Guibert of Nogent, William was "powerful in words", a man who set out to do things too great for him. Guibert said that William was named The Carpenter, not because of his craftsmanship with wood, but because he prevailed in battle like a carpenter, by cutting men down".

Twelfth-century chronicler Robert the Monk stated, "William was of royal stock and was related to Hugh I, Count of Vermandois and Hugh's brother, King Philip I of France." He returned to the Holy Land after the Crusade, and little more is known of his life or death.

There is some speculation that William passed during, or soon after, the end of the First Crusade.

Thus the Carpenter's European lineage (William's noble ancestry) can be traced to the Frankish Duke Ansegisel of Meta Meroving, Poppin II, and Charles Martel. ii

General Charles, "The Hammer", Martel was given credit for leading and winning the "Battle of Tours" in 732. The Battle of Tours, also called the Battle of Poitiers, was fought in north central France, pitting the Frankish and Burgundian forces led by Charles Martel against the Muslim forces led by Abdul Rabman Al Ghafiqi. The Franks were victorious and Charles subsequently extended his authority in the south.

Later, Christian Chroniclers and pre-20th century historians praised Charles Martel as the champion of Christianity, characterizing the battle as the decisive turning point in the struggle against Islam, a struggle which preserved Christianity as the religion of Europe. There is little dispute that the battle lay the foundations for the Carolingian Empire and Frankish domination of Europe for the next century. iii

The ancestral link to "William the Carpenter", makes the Carpenters, called Moytoys by the Cherokees, cousins to the Carpenter Earl of Tyrconnell, and thus related to the current British Royal Family.

Chapter 2 – Arrival in America

Thomas Pasmere Carpenter came to America with the promise of 10 acres in the State of Virginia, by the Secretary of the Colonial Land Office. This parcel was located within the island of James City County, adjoining the land of Mary Bayly.

Upon arrival in Jamestown, Virginia, he was denied access to his promised land due to his age and his decision to live in a cave near the Shawnee Indians. His land grant was transferred to Robert Marshall, September 20, 1628. He was called "Cornplanter" by the Shawnee, derived from their sign language that matched, as near as possible, the work of a carpenter. Thomas married a Shawnee woman named "Pride", who bore a son about 1635 named Trader Carpenter, who later was named Amatoya Moytoy by the Cherokees. iv

Thomas and Pride later gave birth to a daughter named "Pasmere", born about 1637. Pasmere married the grandfather of Cornstalk Hokolesqua (Shawnee) in 1660, and after marriage, died giving birth to their first child, Amoya (Pigeon).

It must be noted here that the historical records which we rely on for the early stories of the Carpenter Family exist only because of Thomas Pasmere Carpenter's insistence that all members of his family learn to read, write, and cipher. Had this not occurred, much of the early Cherokee history would have been lost forever, as their written language was not created until about 1820.

The Cherokee language was written in a syllabary by a silversmith named Sequoyah. The Cherokee Nation officially adopted the syllabary in 1825. Some accounts report that as many as 90% of the Cherokee were literate in their own language by 1830. The traditional way Native Americans passed on history was through story-telling, and to this day this communication technique remains an important method for elders to present history and traditional knowledge to younger tribal members.

The Carpenter family owned several small sailing ships, which were leased to the East India Trading Company, an affiliation dating to the formation of that company on December 31, 1600. Since its creation by Royal Charter, granted by Queen Elizabeth I, the influence of The East India Trading Company has been well documented. It changed the world's taste, its thinking, and its people. Singapore and Hong Kong were established by The Company, and India was shaped and influenced by it.

At one point, The Company had the largest merchant navy in the world and conducted and controlled 50% of world trade. v Records indicate there were as many as fifteen different ships owned by the Carpenter family, those of which were involved with moving furs between the Gulf Ports and Glasgow or Dublin, and trade goods for North America. These ships usually made stops at Barbados, where the family had banking connections set up. These ships were small and fast, often able to make the crossing from Scotland and Ireland in less than thirty days.

Thomas Pasmere Carpenter passed away in 1679 in Running Water Village, Tennessee, and is buried in The Great Mound, Nikwasi, located in Franklin, North Carolina.

The Carpenter family went on to play a very important role in the history of the Cherokee Nation from the mid-1600s well into the late 1700s. During this time period, the Cherokees were located in Eastern Tennessee, North and South Carolina, and Northern Georgia. vi

Chapter 3 - Cherokee Connections

Trader Carpenter, the only son of Thomas Pasmere Carpenter and known as "Amatoya Moytoy I of Chota", became a very dominant character in the early connections between the Carpenter family and the Cherokee Nation. Records indicate he was born in 1635. Trader's first marriage was to Locha of the Shawnee Tribe in 1650. She was the mother of Trader Tom Carpenter, (Amatoya Moytoy II) and a daughter, name unknown.

According to early records, he had three wives, the second and third being from the Cherokee Tribe. Trader Carpenter was known by several different names, which included, "Rain or Water Conjurer", "Amoadaweh", "Amahetai", "Head Warrior of Tellico of the Overhills", "Trader", "Rain Maker", "Amo-adawehi", "CHIEF OF TELLICO", "Beloved Man of Chota", and "SUPREME CHIEF OF THE CHEROKEE". The abundance of names provides a challenge to trace Trader Carpenter's identity through the numerous records.

Although he was married three times and had several children, it was his marriage to QUE-DI-SI of Tellico in 1680 which made the first official connection to the Cherokee lineage. This second marriage produced three sons and eight daughters, several of which played important roles in Cherokee history for over a century. [VII, VIII, IX.]

Records confirm Trader Carpenter had at least thirteen children, even though some accounts claimed over twenty. Two of his offspring were by his first wife, and eleven were from his second marriage to QUE-DI-SI (full blood Cherokee).

Later we will present stories of some of these children who contributed much to early Cherokee history.

Trader Carpenter's third wife's name is unknown. We found no other information about her, except that she was Cherokee, and of the Deer Clan.

Understanding the different Amatoya Moytoys referred to in the historical data is somewhat confusing, but it appears the name was given to the Carpenters based on their ability to witch water.

Reading the different historical accounts would lead one to conclude there were two Amatoya Moytoy I's. However, after careful analysis of time frames, birthdates, marriage dates, and offspring, it becomes clear that Amatoya Moytoy I was, in fact, one person, Trader Carpenter, who had three different wives.

There are no records to indicate what happened to the first wife, Locha, however, records indicate that Trader Carpenter shared a close relationship with the Cherokee Nation, who gave him the name Amatoya Moytoy I.

The name Moytoy (pronounced "Mah-tie") is derived from the Cherokee title Ama Matie.

The confusion arises when A-MA-DO-YA Moytoy, the Indian spelling for Amatoya Moytoy, is listed as a full blood Cherokee in some records. After careful analysis, it becomes apparent that A-MA-DO-YA Moytoy, Trader Carpenter, Amatoya Moytoy I, were all the same person, with his father being of English descent, and his mother a full-blood Shawnee.

11

There are records that suggest it may have been somewhat common when a man, outside the tribe, married a full-blood Cherokee woman, he was considered a full-blood Cherokee, as long as the marriage lasted, and regardless of his blood lineage. This tradition may help explain the confusion that still exists in the historic records as to the identity of Amatoya Moytoy I. Examination of the records suggests that Trader Carpenter lived a very long life.

In 1670, Trader Carpenter and family moved from Chota, Tennessee to Great Tellico, Tennessee, and in 1680, he married QUE-DI-SI, "Nancy" of Tellico (of the Wolf Clan), a full-blood Cherokee. Her Indian name was shortened to Quatsy by the family.

Some of their children include Chief Kanagatoga (Old Hop), Killanera the Butock, Longfellow of Chistatoa, Betsy, Tame Doe, two daughters with unknown names, and Nancy Moytoy.

Nancy Moytoy was the first born and is recorded to be the mother of Chief Attacullakulla, (Little Carpenter). Tame Doe was the mother of Tsistuna-Gis-Ke, (Nancy Ward).

We have been unable to find any information on the other three daughters.

Old Hop, Attacullakulla, and Nancy Ward went on to become very influential in Cherokee history and early American history.

The detailed presentation of this family's marriage and birth records is required in order to clear up the discrepancies found in the existing historic records. Personal stories of these people will appear in later pages (Appendix B, Descendants of William Carpenter, page 1).

Chief Trader Carpenter gained recognition as the "Emperor of the Cherokees" by British envoy Sir Alexander Cummings. The family lost most of their influence when the capital city of Chota-Tanasi, TN, was destroyed by the Continental Army in 1782.

The Carpenters helped establish the towns of Running Water (where Thomas Pasmere Carpenter died in 1675), Nickajack, TN, Lookout Mountain, TN, Crowtown, TN, and Chota, TN. Chota was created as a merging place for people of all tribes, history, and color. It became similar to a capital for the Cherokee Nation. These villages grew to about 2,000 people by 1670, when the Carpenter family moved to Great Tellico.

Here, Trader Carpenter married Quatsy of the Wolf Clan in 1680. This marriage is where the first Cherokee blood lineage entered my heritage.

Trader Carpenter was Chief of all the above mentioned villages and was eventually appointed "Emperor" to represent the Cherokee Nation in all dealings with the British. As one reviews the various records and documents, it becomes apparent that Trader Carpenter was a very dominant figure in Cherokee history during the 1600s.

The historical records also become somewhat confusing, as there were two Trader Tom Carpenters. The first, born in 1660, was the son of Trader Carpenter and Locha, and the second, born in 1687 was the son of Trader Carpenter and his second wife, Quatsy. It was his son, Trader Tom Carpenter by his second wife, Quatsy, who actually became Principal Chief of the Cherokee Nation in 1730. Trader Carpenter died about 1730 and had to have been in his 90s at passing. He is buried at The Great Mound, Nikwasi, Franklin, North Carolina.

It is important we remember it was the off-spring of Trader Carpenter and Quatsy that effectively ruled the Cherokee Nation for over a century. Through his eldest daughter, Nancy Moytoy, Trader Carpenter was the grandfather of Attacullakulla, called the Prince of Chota by the British. He was also the great-grandfather of Nancy Ward. Descendants of Trader Carpenter include the families of Major Ridge, Elias Boudinot, Stand Watie, and Chief Nimrod Jarrett Smith. Information on these important individuals will be presented in later pages.

Trader Carpenter had developed a strong relationship with the British. However, the Cherokees began to favor the French, who had established Fort Toulouse, near present Montgomery, AL. The French showed greater respect for the Indians than the British, who considered them to be an inferior race.

To prevent a Cherokee alliance with the French, Sir Alexander Cummings visited the prominent Cherokee towns and convinced them to select an "Emperor", Chief Moytoy of Tellico (Trader Carpenter) to represent the tribe in all dealings with the British. In addition, he escorted seven Cherokees to England to meet the King and to swear allegiance to the Crown.

Of the seven Cherokees who made the trip, six were offspring of Trader Compenter, Chief of Tellico. The chiefs of the tribe declined to take the trip, due to their responsibilities for hunting and defense.

The information and stories about the Carpenter family were difficult to piece together, but offer much information about the influence the family had on Cherokee history. Fitting the records together has been challenging, as the different sources have provided several discrepancies that required considerable research to unravel.

Continuing the search directs us to focus on Trader Carpenter's first son, Trader Tom Carpenter, the son of Trader Carpenter's first wife, Locha, a full-blood Shawnee.

Again, there is some confusion in the early records, as some accounts list Trader Tom Carpenter's mother as QUE-DI-SI, Trader Carpenter's second wife. Records indicate Trader Tom Carpenter (Amatoya Moytoy II), was born in 1660. Trader Tom Carpenter married "Nancy", a full-blood Shawnee. There are also records showing a Trader Tom Carpenter, born in 1687 to Trader Carpenter and Quatsy. It was the latter Trader Tom Carpenter (Amatoya Moytoy V) that was elected Principal Chief of the Cherokee Nation in 1730.

This scenario seems reasonable, as earlier information indicates the elder Trader Tom Carpenter was active in the family shipping business and made several trips to England. These records also document that Trader Tom Carpenter and his wife, Nancy, moved their residence to Devonshire, England in 1714, to live out their last years, and are buried there. x

Trader Tom Carpenter and his wife, Nancy, raised nine children, five of which were adopted. Their adopted children were Raven of Hiwassee, Waapheti (Swan) Moytoy, Moytoy V (Oshasquia), Old Hop Moytoy, and Tkikami (April) Moytoy. Their birth children were White Owl Raven Carpenter (Moytoy IV), Savannah Tom Carpenter (Moytoy III), Pasmere Carpenter, and Quatsis Carpenter.

By 1710, Chief Moytoy II (Trader Tom Carpenter) eased his second-born son, Savannah Tom Carpenter, into control of Great Tellico, TN, and his first-born son, White Owl Raven Carpenter, into control of the Overhill, TN towns of Upper and Lower Hiwassee, and Old Hop into managing Chota, TN and associated towns. The Moytoy Carpenter family, in the late 1600s, were in full control of the expanding Chickamauga Nation. xi

White Owl Raven Carpenter (Amatoya Moytoy IV) xii

White Owl Raven Carpenter is the ancestral connection for my family lineage. Records clearly show White Owl Raven Carpenter to be the birth son of Trader Tom Carpenter and his wife Nancy, thereby making him half English and half Shawnee. History tells us that Nancy Moytoy, daughter of Trader Carpenter, married Savannah Tom Carpenter and had two daughters, Susan and Elizabeth, and three sons, Great Eagle, Corn Tassel, and Attacullakulla. Savannah Tom Carpenter was killed in battle at a young age, and his wife, Nancy Moytoy, then married White Owl Raven Carpenter.

There appears to be no question that Nancy Moytoy was the mother of Attacullakulla. However, one account suggests that his father was White Owl Raven Carpenter. The most reliable information indicates his father was Savannah Tom Carpenter, and after his father's death, he became the adopted stepson of White Owl Raven Carpenter. This scenario helps explain the confusion in some records that Attacullakulla was adopted and of Algonquin descent. The obvious misinformation is his Algonquin heritage. xiii

White Owl Raven and wife Nancy, had seven children. They were Killaneca, Killaqua, All Bones, Bushyhead, and daughters Betsy, Tame Doe, and Oosta, plus adopted son Amoyah Pigeon. My family lineage comes through Oosta (Wolf Clan), also known as White Owl Great Eagle, who married Alexander Drumgoole. Little information is to be found on Alexander Drumgoole, other than his birth date in 1720 and marriage to Oosta, who is listed as born in 1723. They did have a son, Alexander Drumgoole Sr., born in 1750 and died in 1824. Records show he married Margaret Elizabeth about 1769, Nancy Augusta 1779, Isabella Elliot 1795, and Anna Baltzell 1809. The children of Alexander Drumgoole Sr. and Nancy Augusta were Nannie Drumgoole, 1779, Alexander Wi-HU Drumgoole, 1785, and Ruth Drumgoole 1788. xiv (Appendix B, Descendants of William Carpenter, page 1)

Nancy Augusta was full-blood Cherokee, and some suggest she was a sister to Bushyhead. The Bushyhead name was given to Captain John Stuart, an officer of the British military, because of his heavy growth of

17

blond hair. He married a Cherokee woman, Nancy Foreman, and had one son, also known as Oo-na-du-to (Bushyhead). No records were found to indicate other children.

If there is a connection between Nancy Augusta and the Bushyhead family, it would have been with Oo-na-du-to. The only record that might suggest a link to Nancy Augusta is the fact that Oo-na-du-to's son, Jesse Bushyhead, was educated at the Candy Creek Mission, where Nancy Augusta lived, and he became the first ordained Baptist minister in the Cherokee Nation.

There is an account of the Church at Candy Creek, Cherokee Nation dated January 1828, that states: "Nancy Fields, the aged, having never been able to understand a word of English, has thus not received so much light and instruction as others, and it is painful to state that owing partly to this and partly to prejudice arising from long life of heathenistic practice, her Christian [health] has not been of that uniform [unreadable] character which we had hoped to behold. Yet, we entertain the belief that she is a true believer and (now more than ever before) established in the faith of the gospel. The practice of conjuring and more especially a belief in the [effi-cicy and inoiscency] of the art have constituted the 'right head' in her case which has at length been dropped off. She is rarely able to attend meetings from the distance of half mile; yet whenever her frail nature will permit she is very punctual in her attendance." The Presbyterian Missionary at Candy Creek, William Holland, dubbed her "Nancy Augusta". xv

There is also an interesting story about Nancy's husband, Alexander Drumgoole Sr. in the Papers of the Continental Congress [Microfilm M247, Roll 69] there is the following letter;

Jim

The bearer, Mr. Drumgoole, being here last summer, was instructed with sundry presents from the States and from myself to the principle Indians of the Cherokee Nation, which, as appears by the answers he has now brought to our letters, he faithfully delivered and he interpreted and explained our letters much to the satisfaction of the People. I therefore take leave to mention him to you as a person who from his knowledge of the language and custom of those people, is capable of being useful to the interests of the United States in those parts, if employed understand the superintendants as an agent for Indian affairs. I am informed he is a man of property, and has a good character for [Probity & Zeal] for the public good. As such I recommend him to your [notice] and good counsels, and am, with great esteem.

Your most obedient & most humble servant

B. Franklin [Benjamin Franklin]

This letter is dated December 6, 1787.

This was not Benjamin Franklin's first involvement with Native American interests.

In 1744, Chief Conasatego was a leader of the Onondaga Nation who became a prominent diplomat and spokesman of the Iroquois Confederacy. xvi

He was best known for a speech he gave at the 1744 Treaty of Lancaster, where he recommended that the British colonies emulate the Iroquois by forming a confederacy. Near the end of the conference, Conasatego gave the colonists some advice:

"We have one thing further to say, and that is, We
heartily recommend Union and a Good Agreement
between you, our Brethren. Never disagree.

But preserve a strict Friendship for one another,
and thereby you will be the Stronger.

Our wise Forefathers established Union and
Aminty between the Five Nations (Oneida, Mohawk,
Cayuga and Seneca) (the fifth was added later); this
has made us formidable, this has given us great
weight and Authority with our Neighboring Nations.

We are a Powerful confederacy, and by your
observing the same Methods our wise Forefathers
have taken, you will acquire fresh Strength and
Power; thereby, whatever befalls you, never fall
out with one another." xvii

He made similar recommendations about colonial unity at another
conference in 1745. Historians have claimed that the democratic ideals
of the "Great Law of Peace", of the Iroquois Six Nations (the Tuscarora
added 1722), provided a significant inspiration to Benjamin Franklin,
James Madison, and other framers of the United States Constitution.
Benjamin Franklin and John Adams were invited to visit and study the
Iroquois Federation.

Franklin actually circulated copies of the proceedings of the 1744
Treaty of Lancaster among his fellow colonists. The opening preamble,
"We the people", comes directly from the Iroquois Confederation. In
October 1988, the U. S. Congress passed Concurrent Resolution 331 to

recognize the influence of the Iroquois Constitution upon the American Constitution and Bill of Rights. xviii

The next ancestry link is through Alexander Wi-HU Drumgoole, born in 1785. He married Peggy I-NO-WA-GA-GO-LO-NU-GI, born 1790, who was full-blood Cherokee of the "Wild Potato" Clan. Alexander Wi-HU was two-thirds Cherokee and part Shawnee.

It is important to understand that the clan affiliation was a vital element in the Cherokee society. Cherokee kinship is matrilineal, a unilineal descent rule in which you join your mother's clan at birth, a membership for life. After marriage, it is customary to reside with your wife's clan so your children grow up with their clan, that is, their mother's family. The clan represents a lineage based on a common apical totem ancestor. Marriage, mating, or sexual relationships with a member of the same clan is taboo and considered incest.

Peggy (I-NO-WA-GA-GO-LO-NU-GI) was the first Cherokee name I found. By discovering Peggy's clan affiliation, I could now trace my grandmother, Minerva Courtney Story's clan affiliation to "Wild Potato" [Anigategewi], also called the "Savannah Clan".

Alexander Wi-HU Drumgoole and Peggy had six children. They were George Drumgoole born 1812, Ruth Drumgoole born 1815, Sarah Drumgoole born 1817, Eliza Drumgoole born 1819, Alexander Drumgoole III born 1822, and James Drumgoole born 1824. Sarah Drumgoole went on to marry Samuel Ballard, who was born around 1800. Their daughter, Minerva Ballard, was born 1841, and she married George Washington Countryman, son of John Countryman and Martha Ward.

At this point, we need to go back and open another lineage in my Cherokee ancestry. My journey now takes me back to Trader Carpenter and his wife Quatsy. One of their sons was Old Hop (Standing Turkey), born about 1690, who went on to become Principal Chief of the Cherokee Nation. Old Hop married SU-GI, a full-blood Cherokee of the (Wild Onion) Wolf Clan. They had a daughter named Grasshopper, later known as Granny Hopper, born 1730. xix

One of Old Hop's sister was Nancy Moytoy, the mother of Attacullakulla and another sister was Tame Doe, the mother of Nancy Ward.

It is important to remember that Old Hop, Nancy Moytoy and Tame Doe are all children of Trader Carpenter (Amatoya Moytoy I). Other important people in Cherokee history that link to Trader Carpenter include Major Ridge, referred to as "The Ridge", grandson of Attacullakulla, Stand Watie (Degataga), a Brigadier General of the Confederate States Army during the Civil War, and his brother Buck (Gallagina), who later took the name of Elias Boudinot. The Watie brothers were close to their paternal uncle Major Ridge. Nancy Ward's tie to the Carpenter family is also well documented through Tame Doe, daughter of Trader Carpenter and QUE-DI-SI. (Appendix B, Descendants of William Carpenter, page 2).

It seems important to pause and present some of the interesting stories we have uncovered about several of the early prominent leaders of the Cherokee Nation that are related to the Carpenter family. We have researched and read many accounts of those early leaders, and find one must be very careful in interpreting this information, as there are several discrepancies in the source material.

In our efforts to piece together the historical accounts, we studied family lineage, birth dates, and the source of the information. After months of review, we believe we can provide a reasonably accurate presentation of the facts. The confusion comes primarily from the fact that several of the male family members had more than one wife, and in the 1600s and 1700s it was common practice for Native American families to adopt children that had been orphaned.

Chapter 4 - The Carpenter Influence

Attacullakulla

Nancy Moytoy, known as "Aniwaya Nancy Tenase", was a daughter of Trader Carpenter and QUE-DI-SI, and the mother of Attacullakulla.

Attacullakulla was born about 1699. Records confirm his mother as Nancy Moytoy, but his father raises some question. The best information we found states his father was Savannah Tom Carpenter, birth son of Trader Tom Carpenter and Nancy [Shawnee], who was killed in battle at a young age. Nancy Moytoy then married White Owl Raven Carpenter, Savannah Tom's older brother. White Owl Raven Carpenter was also known as Amatoya Moytoy IV. Based on this data, Attacullakulla became the adopted son of White Owl Raven Carpenter. His name can be interpreted as "Leaning Wood", and he was born in Sevier's Island, Tennessee. He first appears in the written records of 1730. xx

In 1721, a treaty was signed with South Carolina which established a fixed boundary between the Cherokee towns and the colony. To prevent the possible alliance between the French and the Cherokees, Sir Alexander Cumming visited many of the Cherokee towns and convinced the people to select an "Emperor" to represent the tribe. Alexander Cumming later organized a trip to England to meet the King and to swear allegiance to the Crown.

The seven Cherokees that attended were supposedly all chiefs, however, the chiefs refused to go because of their responsibilities to the people. Only one could be considered a prominent Cherokee Chief, the others being young men who went for the adventure.

From 1730 to 1735, Attacullakulla was part of the group of Cherokees who visited London. He was the youngest of the seven who made the voyage. Attacullakulla, known as "Little Carpenter", later became a powerful Cherokee leader and was elected chief. He was considered by many as one of the greatest Cherokees who ever lived.

In 1736, Attacullakulla rejected the advances of the French, who sent emissaries to the Overhill Cherokees. A few years later, he was captured by the Ottawas, allies of the French, who held him captive in Canada until 1748. Upon his return, he became one of the Cherokees' leading diplomats and an advisor to the Beloved Man of Chota, Trader Carpenter.

In May 1759, following a series of attacks by settlers and Cherokees against each other, Attacullakulla, joined a delegation that went to Charleston to try and negotiate with South Carolina authorities.

Governor William Henry Lyttleton seized the delegation as hostages until the Cherokees responsible for killing some white settlers were surrendered. Having put together an expeditionary force, Lyttleton set out for Fort Prince George with the hostages and arrived with a force of 1,700 men on December 9, 1759.

Attacullakulla was freed soon after, but chose to return to Fort Prince George to negotiate for peace. However, his efforts failed as a result of Oconostota's more hawkish attitude. The Cherokees gave up two individuals in trade for the few remaining hostages, which included Oconostota.

Oconostota then enticed Lt. Richard Coytmore from the fort by waving a bridle over his head. Several Cherokee warriors were hiding in the woods and opened fire, killing Coytmore. The white soldiers inside the fort retaliated by murdering all the Cherokees inside, and hostilities between the Cherokees and Anglo-Americans were intensified. xxi

Attacullakulla served as Supreme Chief of the Cherokee Indians from 1761 to 1775. His wife was Nionne Ollie of the Paint Clan, and daughter of Oconostota. They had seven children and two adopted sons. Dragging Canoe was their first born, and became an influential Chief of the Chickamauga Cherokees.

Dragging Canoe was a war leader of a dissident band of young Cherokees against the United States in the American Revolutionary War. He was considered by many to be the most significant leader of the Southeast, providing a significant role model for the younger Tecumseh, who was a member of a band of Shawnee living with the Chickamauga, taking part in their wars. xxii

Attacullakulla's son, Dutsi, also known as Dutch, was the father of Major Ridge and Oowatie. (Appendix B. Descendants of William Carpenter, page 2)

Attacullakulla remained an active leader and negotiator for the Cherokees into the 1770s. When American Revolutionary forces under the command of William Christian occupied the Overhill villages in 1776, Attacullakulla arranged for their withdrawal, and played a leading role in the 1777 peace negotiations at Long Island on Holston. His influence diminished as Dragging Canoe, his son, and other young leaders continued Cherokee resistance to the Americans. Attacullakulla died somewhere between 1780 and 1785. xxiii

Kanagatooga, "Old Hop", "Standing Turkey"

Old Hop was born in 1690 to Trader Carpenter and QUE-DI-SI. He was half-brother to Trader Tom Carpenter, and brother to Nancy Moytoy, Tame Doe, and twenty others. He was of the Wolf Clan and served as Principal Chief of the Cherokees from 1759 until his death August 1, 1761.

Native American historian Fred Gearing described Old Hop as: "When Cherokees had differences among themselves, Old Hop had a great capacity to bring them together. Typically he avoided making decisions himself. He was extremely cool-headed and patient with the more precipitate of the Cherokees around him. In short, Old Hop was the near-perfect embodiment of the Cherokee ideas about proper leadership behavior; that is, unusually circumspect."

It was during the time of his leadership that many Native American tribes were dying of the diseases brought to this continent by the new immigrants. Almost half the population was lost from diseases such as smallpox and measles. This was the time when England was colonizing Virginia and the Carolina commonwealths, in competition with the French.

The name of Old Hop was the result of the fact that he limped due to an injury he sustained as a young warrior. Old Hop was in his elder years when he was chosen as Principal Chief. There are many references to his advanced years throughout the records of time. Old Hop was the uncle of "Attacullakulla" who served as the Peace Chief and spokesman during his time as Chief. Doublehead was Old Hop's brother and served as a chief under Dragging Canoe. He commanded the expedition against Knoxville in 1793, and was killed by Major Ridge.

Old Hop died shortly before the end of the Cherokee-English war of 1760-1761. Little Carpenter announced his death to the council ("Old Frontiers" page 115):

"Our Headman, Old Hop, is gone to sleep, and Standing Turkey is come into his room, but he has little to say, being just come to the government. The other chiefs present will remember how strongly Old Hop recommended to the Nation to live in peace and friendship with the white people."

It is interesting to note that in the old Cherokee culture there were usually three leaders for each town or village; the "War Chief", the "Peace Chief", and a chief similar to a High Priest. In the city of Echota, during this time, the White Chief was Attacullakulla, the Red Chief was Oconostota, and Old Hop was the High Priest.

On page 67 of "Old Frontiers", Old Hop was talking to his brother, Demere, and said the following:

"I am old and lie on a bad bearskin. My life is not more than an inch long, and I know not when a bullet may cut it short. I want my brothers, Captains Demere and Stuart, to remember that the Great Warrior, Oconostota, and his brother [Amo-Scossite?], are the only two men in the Nation that ought to be thought of after my death. It is true that Willenawah and Little Carpenter are my nephews, but I do not know how they would behave. If I had not remembered what I owe to a country I love, and had in mind to behave like a father, I would recommend my two sons, but I know them to be incapable, and biased by every lie that comes. I do not know how they will turn out, but I do know the others, for drunk or sober, they always admonish the Indians to love the white people." XXIV

Nancy Ward

This story is taken from the Tennessee Encyclopedia of History and Culture:

Beloved Woman of the Cherokees, Nancy Ward was born in 1738 at Chota, and given the name Nanye-hi, which means "One who goes about". The name is the legendary name of the Spirit People of Cherokee mythology. Her birth was about the time of a smallpox epidemic that caused the death of nearly half of the Cherokee people. Her father's identity has not been confirmed. However, her mother was Tame Doe, daughter of Trader Carpenter and QUE-DI-SI, and sister to Nancy Moytoy, the mother of Attacullakulla. (Appendix B, Descendants of William Carpenter, page 2)

In her adult years, observers described her as queenly and commanding in appearance and manner as a winsome and resourceful woman. By age seventeen, she had two children, a son, Five Killer, and a daughter, Catherine. Her husband was killed in a raid on the Creeks

31

during the 1755 Battle of Taliwa, where she fought by her husband's side, chewing the bullets for his rifle to make them more deadly. When he fell in battle, she sprang up from behind a log to rally the Cherokee warriors to fight harder. Taking up his rifle, she led a charge that unnerved the Creeks and brought victory to the Cherokees.

Because of her valor, the clans chose her as Ghighau, "Beloved Woman of the Cherokees". In this powerful position, her words carried much weight in the tribal government, because the Cherokees believed that the Great Spirit frequently spoke through a Beloved Woman. As Beloved Woman, Nanye-hi headed the Women's Council and sat on the Council of Chiefs. She had complete power over prisoners. Sometimes known as Agi-ga-u-e-or, "War Woman", she also prepared the warriors Black Drink, a sacred ritual preparatory to war.

Bryant Ward, an Irish trader who had fought in the French and Indian War, took up residence with the Cherokees and married Nancy in the late 1750s. Ward had an Irish wife, but since Cherokees did not consider marriage a lifelong institution, the arrangement presented few problems. Nancy Ward and her Irish husband lived in Chota for a time and became the parents of a daughter, Betsy. Eventually Bryant Ward moved back to South Carolina where he lived the remainder of his life with his white wife and family. Nancy Ward and Betsy visited his home on many occasions, where they were welcomed and treated with respect.

Nancy Ward also became respected and well known by the settlers moving across the mountains into Cherokee territory. John Sevier owed much of his military success to her. On at least two occasions, she sent Isaac Thomas to warn Sevier of impending Indian attacks.

She once stopped the warriors of Toqua from burning Lynda Bean at the stake. Ward kept Bean, the wife of Tennessee's first permanent settler, at her home for a time before allowing her to return to Watauga. Ward made good use of the white woman's enforced stay and learned the art of making butter and cheese. Subsequently, Ward bought cattle and introduced dairying to the Cherokees.

Ward exerted considerable influence over the affairs of both the Cherokees and the white settlers, and participated actively in treaty negotiations.

In July 1781, she spoke powerfully at the negotiations held on the Long Island of the Holston River following settler attacks on Cherokee towns. Oconastota designated Kaiya-tahee (Old Tassel) to represent the Council of Chiefs in the meeting with John Sevier and the other treaty commissioners.

After Old Tassel finished his persuasive talk, Ward called for a lasting peace on behalf of both white and Indian women. This unparalleled act of permitting a woman to speak in the negotiating council took the commissioners back.

In their response, Colonel William Christian acknowledged the emotional effects her plea had on the men and praised her humanity, promising to respect the peace, if the Cherokees likewise remained peaceful.

Ward's speech may have influenced the negotiators in a more fundamental way, because the resulting treaty was one of the few where settlers made no demand for Cherokee land. Before the meeting, the commissioners had intended to seek all land north of the Little Tennessee River.

Nevertheless, the earlier destruction of Cherokee towns and the tribe's winter food supply left many Indians facing hunger. As a result of the desperate circumstances, Ward and the very old Oconastota spent the winter in the home of Joseph Martin, Indian Agent to the Cherokees and husband of Ward's daughter, Betsy.

Again at the Treaty of Hopewell in 1785, Ward made a dramatic plea for continued peace. At the close of the ceremonies, she invited the commissioners to smoke her pipe of peace and friendship.

Wistfully hoping to bear more children to people of the Cherokee Nation, Ward looked to the protection of Congress to prevent future disturbances and expressed the hope that the "chain of friendship will never more be broken".

Although the commissioners promised that all settlers would leave Cherokee lands within six months, and even gave the Indians the right to punish recalcitrant homesteaders, whites ignored the treaty, forcing the Cherokees to make additional land concessions.

During the 1790s, Ward came to be known as Granny Ward, because she took in and provided for a number of children. At the same time, she observed enormous changes taking place within the Cherokee Nation as the Indians adopted the commercial agricultural lifestyle of the nearby settlers and pressed for a republican form of government. Unlike the old system of clan and tribal loyalty, the new Cherokee government provided no place for a "Beloved Woman".

The Hiwassee Purchase of 1819 forced Ward to abandon Chota. She moved south and settled on the Ocoee River near present day Benton, Tennessee. There she operated an inn on the Federal Road until her death in 1822. Her grave is located on a nearby hill beside the graves of

Five Killer and her brother Long Fellow (The Raven). A monument was erected on her grave in 1923 by the Nancy Ward Chapter, Daughters of the American Revolution. xxv

Chapter 5 - The Removal and Treaty of Echota

Ka-nun–tla-cla-geh, Major Ridge

Major Ridge was born in 1771 in the village of Hiawasee, Tennessee. His father, Dutsi, also called Dutch, was the son of Attacullakulla, and his mother was E-li-si of the Deer Clan.

Ka-num-tla-cla-ghe, "The Man Who Walks the Mountain Tops", was called the "Ridge" by the whites, and later became known as

Major Ridge for his participation in the Creek War of 1813 to 1814. He was the leader of the Ridge or Treaty Party.

His brother, Oo-wa-tie, "The Ancient One", was the father of Stand Watie. The Ridge was the grandson of Attacullakulla, the High Chief of the Cherokees.

When Ridge was ten or eleven, his father moved the family to Chestowee, not far from Hiwassee. They became part of the group headed by Dragging Canoe that broke with the Cherokee Council in 1775. The federal government later destroyed the power of the Chicamauga group, and the group asked to be reinstated in the Cherokee Council.

In his teens, Ridge was known for his athletic prowess, particularly in stick ball. All the time, only men with the greatest ability were selected by the tribe to participate in the matches, as they were often played to settle clan and inter-tribal disputes.

In his early twenties, he married Srhoya, also known as Susannah Wickett, and moved to a town named Pine Log, in what is now Georgia. They built a two-story home on a bluff near the Ooatanaula River, which is now the Chieftain's Museum, a National Landmark on the Trail of Tears Historic Trail.

They soon moved to an area close to Pine Log, The Head of Coosa, where Ridge became a slave-owner, growing cotton, corn, grains, and grass for cattle and horses on his plantation. Records indicate his holdings included 1141 peach trees, 418 apple trees, 280 acres under cultivation, a ferry, a store, 30 black slaves and other slaves including Creek captives.

Major Ridge's brother was David-Oo-Watie, who had a son known as Buck Watie. Buck was educated in Cornwall, Connecticut, at the Foreign Mission School, receiving financial assistance from Dr. Elias Boudinot from New Jersey, a member of the U. S. Congress and Director of the U. S. Mint. In return, Buck agreed to accept the doctor's name as his own.

While at the mission, Buck met Samuel Worcester, a missionary. Worcester subsequently requested that his next mission be to the Cherokees. Upon his arrival, Elias (Buck) asked for Worcester's help in establishing a Cherokee newspaper. Elias Boudinot thus became the first editor of the Cherokee newspaper. The Cherokee Phoenix, established 1828, is currently the oldest newspaper in the United States.

Major Ridge's other nephew was Stand Watie, the younger brother of Elias. Stand served as a Confederate General in the Civil War and was the last general to surrender in that war. (Appendix B, Descendants of William Carpenter, page 1)

Major Ridge was the father of Walter Ridge, John Ridge, Sarah "Sallie" Paschal, and Nancy Ridge. In 1818, Nancy Ridge died in childbirth. That same year, John was sent to join his cousin, Elias, at the mission school. About 1822, John married Sarah Bird Northrup, nicknamed Sally, of Cornwall, Connecticut. In 1826, he became licensed as an attorney.

Also in 1826, Major Ridge enlarged his home, which became known as the Ridge Mansion. The mansion had four fireplaces, eight paneled rooms, and thirty Grecian-style columns. The operation of the plantation and mansion required thirty servants.

In 1830, John and Sally gave birth to a son, John Rollin Ridge, ("Yellow Bird"). Attorneys John Ridge and his cousin Elias Boudinot visited our nation's capitol on January 15, 1831, and met with members of the 21st Congress, Second Session. Andrew Jackson was President at the time.

A delegation from the Cherokee Nation presented a "Memorial" [Doc. No. 57], written by John Ridge, Elias Boudinot, R. Taylor, and

W.S. Coodey, and was published in the Congressional Record for that day.

I have an original copy of this Section of the Congressional Record, which was found in an antique shop in the small community of Mecosta, Michigan. This shop was located in an old church building which is over one hundred years old and was part of the Underground Railroad System in the 1800s. There were numerous tunnels under the basement of the building where escaped slaves hid, in their effort to enter into Canada.

The Cherokee Principal Chief's Office photographed the document during my visit to Tahlequah in 2011. This memorial is to respectfully call attention to a matter of great concern to the Cherokee people. It points out that the State of Georgia, in its desire to acquire the extent of her chartered limits, set forth a claim to a large portion of Cherokee lands, as having been purchased under the treaty of "Indian Springs", made with the Creek Nation. The record states that this treaty was made null and void by a new treaty of 1826 made in Washington D.C.

It further states on the portion of land they have been deprived of, were the homes of many Cherokees who have been compelled to leave them, including their farms that afforded their families subsistence.

The record concludes: "We implore that our people may not be denounced as savages, unfit for the GOOD NEIGHBORHOOD, guaranteed to them by treaty. Between the compulsive measures of Georgia and our destruction we ask the interposition of your authority, and a remembrance of the bond of perpetual peace pledged for our safety, thus safety of the last fragments of once mighty nations, that have gazed for a while upon your civilization and prosperity, but which now totter on the brink of angry billows, whose waves have covered in oblivion other nations that were once happy, but are no more!" (Appendix "A" is a copy of the Congressional Record)

In 1829, President Andrew Jackson called for the Congress to enact legislation to remove Native American tribes living east of the Mississippi River, to lands set aside for them west of the Mississippi River. The white civilization had determined they could no longer tolerate Native American lands in the Eastern United States, as it was preventing the progress and development of their culture.

On May 28, 1830, President Jackson signed the new legislation into law. In the beginning, Major Ridge did not support selling tribal lands to the U. S. Government. In 1830, the U. S. Supreme Court ruled the Territory of Georgia's Indian Code as unconstitutional. However, President Jackson refused to enforce the Supreme Court ruling. After Jackson's refusal, Samuel Marshall resigned himself to the Cherokee's eventual forced movement west.

The Cherokee supporters in Congress now believed their cause to be hopeless. John Ridge conveyed his own dismay to his father and recommended the Cherokees accept the new treaty for lands west of Arkansas offered by the U. S. Secretary of War, Lewis Cass. Major Ridge long opposed the new government proposals for the Cherokees to sell their land and move west.

However, the rapidly expanding white settlement, and Georgia's efforts to abolish the Cherokee government, caused him to change his mind. Based on advice from his son, Major Ridge, came to believe the best way to preserve the Cherokee Nation was to get good terms for their lands from the U. S. Government before it was too late.

On December 22, 1835, Ridge was one of the signers of the Treaty of New Echota, which exchanged the Cherokee tribal lands east of the Mississippi River for land in what is today Oklahoma.

The treaty was of questionable legality, and was rejected by Chief John Ross and most of the Cherokee people. Nevertheless, the treaty was ratified by the U. S. Senate. Signers of the treaty included the Ridges, Elias Boudinot, Stand Watie, and John Ross's brother, Andrew (who initially proposed the removal process). xxvi

The treaty was declared illegally executed by the Cherokee Council. In 1837, Major Ridge and John settled their families in Indian Territory close to Honey Creek, which was a tributary of the Neosho River, and only minutes from the Missouri border. They began to clear the land and plant apple, peach, and a few cherry and pear trees. The Major and John also built a store on Honey Creek. Elias Boudinot and his new bride settled close to the new town of Park Hill.

By 1828, the Cherokees were not nomadic savages. In fact, they had assimilated many European-style customs, including the wearing of gowns by Cherokee women. They built roads, schools, and churches, had a system of representational government, and were farmers and cattle ranchers.

The Cherokees actually must be given credit for the very first public school in America. Literacy was high in the Cherokee Nation following the development of the syllabary by Sequoyah, and the establishment of a newspaper printed in two languages in the 1820s. In the 1890s, literacy among the Cherokees was higher than citizens of Arkansas or Texas.

In 1851, a school for women opened and was the first higher education facility for women west of the Mississippi. Studies included Latin, botany, chemistry, physics and music. xxvii

I was told that my Grandmother Minerva attended the Cherokee Seminary, although I was unable to find documentation of her enrollment.

John Ross opposed the Treaty of Echota, as did most of the Cherokee people. This treaty was ratified by the U. S. Senate by just one vote, and the forced removal of the Cherokees began as was promised by the government to Georgia in 1802. General John Wool resigned in protest, and was replaced by General Winfred Scott, who arrived at New Echota May 17, 1838 with 7,000 men.

Early that summer, General Scott and the U. S. Army began the invasion of the Cherokee Nation. One of the saddest episodes of our brief history, was how men, women, and children were taken from their land, herded into makeshift forts with minimal facilities and food, then forced to march a thousand miles. The indifference of the Army commanders resulted in very high loss of human life to the first groups of Cherokees.

John Ross made an urgent plea to Scott, requesting that the general let his people lead the tribe west. General Scott agreed, and Ross organized the tribe into smaller groups and let them move separately through the wilderness so they could forage for food. Although the parties under Ross left in early fall and arrived in Indian Territory during the winter of 1838-1839, he significantly reduced the loss of life among his people. Still, close to 4,000 Cherokees died making the journey, a journey that became known as "The Trail of Tears" [Nunna dual Tsuny].

There is an old Oklahoma legend called the Cherokee Rose as retold by S. E. Schlosser:

"We lost everything after the treaty was signed. The white men wanted the Indians removed, and so we were removed. We lost our homes, our sacred lands, our way of life. We were thrust out by greed, and our hearts broke on the long, long journey west. We only had the few precious belongings we could carry, and many of us were forced into camps and then marched west.

"The weather turned cold, and still we marched, without adequate shelter, without blankets. Our men were grim with anger and pain. Our children were crying for comfort we could not give. Many were dying. And we women, we wept. Our hearts were broken. Our spirits were drowning in pain. Our hope was gone. Such terrible grief made us neglect our families, our appearance. We were ready to die rather than go another step.

"Seeing our pain, the Elders gathered together and began praying that some sign would come to ease the heart-numbing horror we felt at our loss, so that we might once again care for our children, comfort their tears, and walk proudly beside our men during this terrible journey. And the Elders were answered.

"The very next morning as we began our long hard journey once again, we began to see white roses growing along the trail. They seemed to have sprung up overnight, and they were very beautiful. The pedals of each rose were white like our tears. The center was yellow like the gold the greedy white men took from our hills. And we counted seven leaves on each stem just as there were seven clans in the Cherokee Nation! The sight of the roses brought a strange peace into the hearts of the Cherokee women who saw them. There was a particularly large patch of them in a small glen where many of us had sat weeping the previous night. I paused to pick one, and one of the Elders stopped beside me and told me there was a rose for each tear we had shed during the journey. His words stayed with me as I took up my parcel of belongings, hurried my children into line, and set out behind my husband. A rose for every tear. Could it be possible? In my heart, I already believed him.

"It was a small wonder. A tiny miracle. But the best parts of our lives are made up of small miracles and tiny wonders. It gave us heart. Though we suffered much in the rest of the journey to Oklahoma Territory—a journey later called the Trail of Tears—and though we lost many children along the way, somehow we had hope that a better day was coming for the Cherokee. And so it has."

But the Cherokee rose continues to grow along the route of the trail today, as a reminder of the past and a hope for the future. xxiii

Certainly, the Trail of Tears was one of the black marks in our American history, and will never be forgotten.

John Ross arrived in Indian Territory in 1839. Upon arrival, he attempted to take over the government from the earlier settlers, but was unsuccessful. Several dozens of Ross's followers met and invoked the blood laws, calling for the death of Major Ridge, John Ridge, Elias Boudinot, and four others.

That night, assassins dragged John Ridge from his bed and Joseph Spears took his life. The next morning, as he was leaving Samuel

Worchester's home, assassins stabbed Elias in the back and killed him. A Choctaw, who witnessed the assassination, rode Worchester's horse to warn Stand Watie, who escaped on the same horse.

That same morning, Major Ridge was on his way to Van Buren, Arkansas. The assassins—James Foreman, Bird Doublehead, two of the Springstons, James Hair, Johnston, Money Talker, Joseph Beanstalk, and Soft Shell Turtle—hid in the underbrush at a place where the road crossed Little Rock Creek. In the ambush, they fired five shots into The Ridge, killing him.

It is important to note that neither of Ross's two relatives who signed the treaty, were assassinated.

At first historians had unkind words for the Ridge family and the Treaty Party. Today, historians are now saying that the actions of the Treaty Party may have saved the Cherokee people from total destruction, which the Yemassee and several other essentially dead tribes suffered.

Major Ridge is buried at the Polson Cemetery in the northwest corner of Oklahoma, near Southwest City, Missouri. His son, John, his wife, and Stand Watie, are also buried there. I had the opportunity to visit the cemetery in 2013. xxix, xxx, xxxi

As the Ridge family involvement in Cherokee history closes, there is no better symbol of the pain and suffering of the "Trail Where They Cried", than the Cherokee Rose. The story of the "Cherokee Rose" has been told many times, but we must never forget this tragedy that remains a shameful event in our American history. Unfortunately, the "Removal Act of 1830" effected many other eastern tribes along with the Cherokees.

Some tribes totally disappeared as a result of Indian removal efforts. Although there is no firm documentation, there are estimates that as many as 15,000 members of the eastern tribes may have lost their lives during the removal enforcement period. To this day, the Cherokee rose thrives along the route of the "Trail of Tears." xxxii, xxxiii

Chapter 6 - Indian Territory (Oklahoma) Settlement

Stand Watie

Stand Watie was born December 12, 1806 in Oothcaloga, Cherokee Nation (currently Calhoun, Georgia). He was the son of David Uwatie, a full-blood Cherokee and Susanna Reese, daughter of a white father and Cherokee mother. Stand Watie's Cherokee name was Degataga, meaning "Stand Firm". He was a leader of the Cherokee Nation and a Brigadier General of the Confederate States Army during the American Civil War. He commanded the Confederate Indian Calvary of the Army of the Trans-Mississippi, made up mostly of Cherokee, Muskogee, and Seminole, and was the final Confederate General in the field to surrender at the end of the war.

Buck Watie (Elias Boudinot)

Prior to the removal of the Cherokees to Indian Territory in 1838, Watie and his older brother, Buck Watie (Elias Boudinot) were among the leaders who signed the Treaty of New Echota in 1835.

By 1827, their father, David Uwatie, had become a wealthy plantation owner who had slaves.

After Uwatie converted to Christianity with the Moravians, he took the name of David and renamed his son Degataga as Isaac. Degataga preferred to use the English translation of his Cherokee name, Stand Firm.

Later, the family dropped the U from their name, using Watie. Along with his two brothers and his sisters, Stand learned to read and write English at the Moravian Mission School in Spring Place, Georgia. The Moravian Church, known as the "Unity of the Brethren", is one of the oldest Protestant denominations in the world, with its heritage dating back to the Bohemian Reformation in the fifteenth century. The church name comes from the exiles that came to Saxony from Moravia, to escape persecution, but its heritage actually started in 1457 in Kunvald, Bohemia, a spate kingdom within the Holy Roman Empire.

Today, church membership numbers about 750,000 and continues their focus on missionary work. xxxiv

The Watie family, along with several other Cherokees, moved to Indian Territory several years before the Trail of Tears. They were known as the "Old Settlers". The "Old Settlers" Roll of 1851 was a listing of Cherokee still living in 1851, who were already residing in Indian Territory when the main body of the Cherokee arrived in the winter of 1839—as a result of the Treaty of Echota, signed in 1835.

Approximately one third of the Cherokee people at that time were Old Settlers, and two thirds were new arrivals. xxxv

In 1842, Watie recognized James Foreman as one of his brother's executioners and murdered him. This was part of the post Removal violence within the tribe, which was close to civil war for years. Ross supporters executed Stand's brother, Thomas, in 1845.

At least 34 politically related murders were committed among the Cherokees in 1845 and 1846.

In 1850, Stand Watie was tried in Arkansas for the murder of Foreman, and was found not guilty on the basis of self-defense. His nephew, Elias Cornelius Watie, who had been educated as an attorney in the East, defended him.

Watie developed a successful plantation on Spavinaw Creek in the Indian Territory. He served on the Cherokee Council from 1845 to 1861, and part of the time served as Speaker. After Ross fled to federally controlled territory in 1862, Watie replaced Ross as Principal Chief.

Watie was one of only two Native Americans on either side in the Civil War that rose to the rank of Brigadier General. The other was Ely S. Parker, a Seneca who fought on the Union side. A military memorial was erected at the Poulson Cemetery to honor Stand Watie's military career.

John Ross had signed an alliance with the Confederacy in 1861 to avoid disunity within his tribe and among the Indian Territory Indians. Within a year, he and part of the National Council concluded the agreement was disastrous.

In 1862, Ross removed the tribal records to Union-held Kansas, and proceeded to Washington to meet with President Lincoln. After Ross's departure, Tom Pegg took over as Principal Chief of the Pro-Union Cherokees.

Following President Lincoln's Emancipation Proclamation in January 1863, Pegg called a special session of the Cherokee National Council. February 18, 1863, the Council passed a resolution to emancipate all slaves within the boundaries of the Cherokee Nation. Most of the "freed" slaves were held by Pro-Confederate Cherokees, so they did not gain immediate freedom.

Stand Watie pushed for recognition of a separate "Southern Cherokee Nation", but never achieved it. The U. S. Government refused to recognize the divisions the Cherokees suggested for adopting the former slaves into the tribe. The Cherokees wanted the government to give the Freedmen an exclusive piece of associated territory. The federal government required that the Cherokee Freedmen receive full rights for citizenship, land, and annuities as the Cherokees.

In the Treaty of 1866, the government declared John Ross as the rightful Principal Chief. The tribe was strongly divided over the treaty issues and the return of John Ross.

In 1867, a new Chief was elected, Lewis Downing, a full-blood and considered a compromise candidate.

Shortly after Downing's election, Stand Watie returned to the Nation where he tried to stay out of politics and rebuild his fortune. Returning to Honey Creek, he died September 9, 1871 and was buried in the old Ridge Cemetery, later called Polson's Cemetery. xxxvi, xxxvii

Elias Boudinot was assassinated in 1839, but must be recognized as the first editor of the Cherokee Phoenix newspaper. This newspaper today is still being published, and is the oldest newspaper in the United States, now in its 187th year. xxxviii

Nimrod Jarrett Smith

Nimrod Jarrett Smith (1837-1893), or Tsaladihi, was the fourth Principal Chief of the Eastern Cherokee Band. His father was Henry Smith, one of the wealthiest men in the Eastern Band of the Cherokees. Nimrod Smith was also the great-grandson of David Watie and therefore the great-grand-nephew of Major Ridge, first cousin of John Ridge, and grand-nephew of Stand Watie and Elias Boudinot through his paternal grandmother, Sarah Susan Watie. He was well known by his Cherokee name, Tsaladihi, which was an attempt to render in

54

Cherokee his middle name, Jarrett, which he was frequently addressed by.

During the American Civil War, Nimrod served the Confederacy as First Sergeant of B Company in the Cherokee Battalion of Thomas' Legion of Cherokee Indians and Highlanders, under the command of then Principal Chief William Holland Thomas.

A well educated and well-spoken man, he was fluent in both Cherokee and English, although he learned Cherokee as a second language. He was elected Principal Chief in 1880, after the death of Principal Chief Lloyd Welch.

As Principal Chief, Nimrod exercised unprecedented power over and influence among the Eastern Cherokee. He aggressively worked to gain official U. S. Government recognition for the Eastern Band as a tribe under the federal law. His efforts were rewarded with a successful conclusion. Chief Smith was a radical anti-assimilationist, fighting against acculturation into the white American society. He was also chiefly responsible for the incorporation of the Eastern Band as a legal entity by the North Carolina legislature. xxxix

The historical records of prominent Cherokee people and the connection to important European History provided several interesting stories, but we now must turn to the connection of two branches of the Carpenter family, which came together with the birth of my great-grandmother, Ann Eliza (Countryman) Courtney.

The Drumgoole branch records the birth of Sarah Drumgoole in 1817, who married Samuel Ballard, born 1800. Sarah was the daughter of Alexander Wi-Hu Drumgoole and Peggy I-NO-WA-GA-GO-LO-

NU-GI. Samuel and Sarah had a daughter, Minerva Ballard, born 1841 XL (Appendix B, Descendants of William Carpenter, page 1)

The other branch begins with the marriage of John Ward to Catherine McDaniel, daughter of Granny Hopper. The son of John and Catherine was George Ward, whose daughter was Martha Ward. Martha married John Countryman and had several children. One of their sons, George Washington Countryman, born in 1839, married Minerva Ballard.

George Washington Countryman and three of his brothers were part of the Second Cherokee Mounted Volunteers in 1862. This group was part of Stand Watie's troops during the Civil War. The three brothers were: Andrew, John, and Samuel Countryman. George Washington Countryman was my great-great grandfather.

George and his wife Minerva are buried in the Ballard-Countryman Cemetery near Bernice, Oklahoma. I have also had the opportunity to visit this cemetery. (Appendix B, Descendants of William Carpenter, page 1)

My great-grandmother was Ann Elisa Countryman, daughter of George Washington Countryman and Minerva Ballard. Ann was born in 1863 and married John L. Courtney, born in 1851. John was not of Native American descent. He and Ann lived in Miami, Oklahoma.

Ann passed in 1941 and is buried at the Mount Hope Cemetery in Afton, Oklahoma. We were able to visit Mount Hope Cemetery where John L. is buried on the Courtney family plot next to his wife. John and Ann had three daughters, the youngest being born in 1886 and died in 1920. Minerva married Otho M. Story Sr., the son of James Alexander Story and Frances Dalton. James and Frances had a large family with four sons and nine daughters. (Appendix B, Pedigree: Otho Miller Story, Jr., page 1).

Lulu Courtney, Minerva Story (holding Dad),
Great-Grandmother Courtney, and Dad's sister, Nadean

The best information available indicates the Story family came to Indian Territory from Tennessee. When the Story family moved on from Oklahoma to California, Otho chose to remain in Oklahoma. When Minerva passed away, her mother, Ann Elisa Courtney, assumed the responsibility for raising Minerva's three children, as Otho was employed as a switchman for the Frisco Railroad Company, and had limited time to raise a family. Otho Jr. was the youngest of the children and stayed with his grandparents the longest. Leota and Nadean stayed with their grandparents until they were old enough to help keep house for their father. My father, Otho M. Story Jr., married Floy Mae Bell, his high school friend, and I was the only child.

Years later, during a visit with my Aunt Leota, she recalled that her mother, being ill with the flu, asked the family to bring her babies to her so she could see them, knowing she had little time left to live. She stated, "Be sure to take good care of my babies for me." This story signifies a mother's love, and also amplifies the similarity between two cultures that believe there is life after death.

Mom's family is linked to the Bell and Meek families, and records document the Bell side of the family goes back to the 1700s. The Bell family has also played an important role in settling Indian Territory and Oklahoma.

Prior to arrival in America there was a Scottish branch and an English branch of the Bell family that had common ancestry. Alexander Bell, born 1760, came to this country in late 1700s from Scotland. There is no record of his marriage, but a son, Samuel Bell, was born in 1783, who married Elizabeth Crider, born in 1787. This family of Bells made many contributions to our country in military and political affairs.

John Bell was a Senator in Tennessee when the Civil War broke out, and cast the deciding vote that the State would fight with the South. One Bell ancestor was a member of the Virginia Regiment during the Revolutionary War, and several others fought in the Civil War.

Eventually, the Bell family connected to the Skeen family through a marriage in 1877. James Samuel Bell and Dorthulie Bell were the parents of my grandfather, Walter Edd Bell, born in 1886 in Nashville, Tennessee. In 1900, the Bell Family moved from Texas to Indian

Territory and started a lumber mill on the Blue River. (Appendix B, Pedigree - Floy Mae Bell, pages 1 thru 5)

I found little information on the Meek family's early history. My great-grandfather and great-grandmother were Jesse Preston Meek and Mary Minerva Craig. Both were born in Kentucky and in 1866 they were married in Clay County, Illinois. Soon after their marriage, they moved to Texas and raised ten children.

The youngest of these children was my grandmother, Mattie Minerva, born in 1890.

Jesse Meek fought in the Civil War and, according to family information, is buried in the Fort Gibson Military Cemetery, in Oklahoma.

Mattie married Walter Edd Bell in 1908. They raised two daughters, one of which was my mother. XLI

I have uncovered my family ancestry from numerous records, documents, and a variety of other sources. It has afforded a whole new appreciation for the Native American culture and a pride in my ancestry I never understood before.

The traditional knowledge of this culture and the strong spirituality of the people offers opportunities for our modern Western culture to emulate.

Probably the most intriguing realization has been the appreciation for the Native American culture's ability to observe the detail of creation. The Cherokee people seem to prefer to remain close to nature and understand the complexity of our surroundings and the relationships that connect us to all living things.

Learning to live in balance with nature is a lesson we need, and can be achieved by sharing with each other. Tribal members shared a strong remembrance of the tribulations and achievements of the Cherokee Nation.

The other exciting experience we have encountered is the reaction of some people that have reviewed this manuscript. One person stated, "Your report has changed our outlook on Native Americans. We confess we didn't know they included lawyers, members of Congress and generals in the Army on both sides of the Civil War. We blame our schools for our ignorance."

Chapter 7 - The Cherokee Way

This has been an incredible journey and presenting a brief history about the Cherokee people, their culture, origin, and traditional beliefs, provides a fitting conclusion to the story.

The Cherokee are a people considered to be indigenous to North America who, at the time of European contact in the 16th century, inhabited what is now the eastern and southeastern United States, before most were forcefully moved to the Ozark Mountains. The society traditionally was divided into seven clans, and their government consisted of three units, each headed by a chief.

The three government divisions were the White Chief, the Red Chief, and the Spiritual Chief, or Medicine Chief, who resolved disagreements between the Red and White Chiefs.

The seven clans were a social organization based on the maternal lineage of the mother. It was strictly forbidden to marry within your clan, which served to prevent genetic problems for the society.

The number seven was also sacred to the Cherokee from ancient times. The Cherokee had a matrilineal society, a social system in which their descent was strictly based on the mother's side of the family. The most important man in the life of any child was their mother's brother. Discipline and instruction in hunting and warfare was not the father's responsibility, but was the responsibility of their maternal uncle. [XLII]

The present day capitol of the Cherokee Nation is Tahlequah, Oklahoma. According to the local legend, after the arrival of the Cherokee people from the Trail of Tears, the three Chiefs scheduled a meeting near the current location of Tahlequah, to select a site to establish a new government. When they arrived, only two of the three were on time. After waiting for sometime, the two chiefs approved and named the site. "Tahle" is interpreted as the number 2, and "quah" translates to it's enough.

The White government consisted of the Chief and Deputy, plus counselors [one from each clan], a Council of Elders, a Chief Speaker and a Council of Grandmothers. This group represented the decision makers during peacetime.

The Red government involved a Great Red War Chief, a second Leader, seven War Counselors, a Chief War Speaker, messengers, Ceremonial Officers, and War Scouts. The seven War Counselors were responsible for determining when it was necessary to declare war.

One interesting twist is that the Council of Grandmothers declared the fate of captives and prisoners taken in wartime.

The Cherokee, as well as many Native American tribes, believed in the ancient custom of blood revenge. It was believed this custom would restore balance of the forces between the two worlds, the spirit world and the world of physical reality, thereby releasing the soul of the victim, to let them pass from this world to the next. The Ancient Law of Blood Revenge was abolished by the Cherokee National Government on September 11, 1808.

The seven Cherokee clans are:

Blue Clan, [a-ni-so-ho-ni] Makers of the Cherokee black drink for purification ceremonies.

Long Hair Clan, [ah-ni-gi-lo-hi] The Peace Chief was usually from this clan.

Bird Clan, [a-ni-tsi-s-qua] Keepers of the birds. Skilled hunters of birds.

Paint Clan, [a-ni-wo-di] Makers of red paint and gatherers of sacred colors for ceremonies.

Deer Clan, [a-ni-a-wi] Known as fast runners and skilled deer hunters.

Wild Pototo Clan, [a-ni-ga-do-ge-wi] Gatherers of the wild potato and food.

Wolf Clan, [a-ni-wa-ya] Largest and most prominent clan providing most of the Red War Chiefs.

The seven clans are frequently mentioned in the ritual prayers and even in the written laws of the tribe. They also seem to have some connection to the "seven mother towns" of the Cherokee. The ancient Cherokee believed there are seven levels of spiritual attainment or achievement, and each clan represents one of these levels. The clans and their members simply represent a balance of the spiritual forces that made up the world of the "Real People'. All members of the society were viewed as equal. XLIII

I have a particular interest in the "Wild Potato" Clan as that is the clan my grandmother belonged to. They were also called the Bear Clan, the Savannah Clan, and the Raccoon Clan. The members of this clan were the "keepers of Mother Earth", and were the gatherers and farmers. Their responsibilities were to gather, develop, maintain, and teach the knowledge and introspection of gathering, growing, preserving food, and providing shelter. Members of this clan were nurtures by nature. XLIV

The origins of the indigenous people of the American continent has been a subject of much research and speculation over the years. When I was taking courses in American history, we were taught that the various Native American tribes came to this continent by way of the land bridge that once connected Siberia to Alaska.

Today anthropologists have discovered information that suggests the several hundred tribes that exist on this continent probably arrived by several different routes. Evidence has been found that supports the South Pacific Island people, thousands of years ago, had the capability of navigating long distances from island to island, and apparently made it to the western shores of South America, and as far north as current California.

Recent discoveries of stone-age technology in southern France, indicates ties to similar technology on the North American continent. This information has lead to speculation that some of the Paleo-Indians may have followed the receding ice in primitive boats or by walking on the ice to reach the North American continent. Archeological finds in the United States dates the ancestors of our indigenous people back to at least 30,000 years ago.

Some tribes, including members of the Anishnaabe Nation, believe their ancestors came from the earth and originated on this continent in the northeastern U. S. and southeast Canada along the Great Salt Sea to the East.

Chapter 8 - Cherokee Origin

The story of the Cherokee origin has produced two different theories. However, time frames cannot be defined, and it may well be the different stories are connected and are simply one complete story.

The first theory is presented by historians and ethnographers, suggesting the Cherokee speak in Iroquoian style language, and therefore are believed to have split off from the Iroquois Nation. This conclusion indicates in ancient times they migrated south from the Great Lakes area. They settled in the southeastern U. S. in North Carolina, South Carolina, Georgia, and eastern Tennessee areas, until forcibly removed to Indian Territory, which today is Oklahoma.

The Cherokee history class, supported by the Cherokee Nation, presents a somewhat different story of their origin. Their story suggests that the people originated from an island somewhere off the coast of South America. It tells of a land surrounded by undrinkable water, how they sacrificed from temples, how the earth shook, and the mountain tops opened up and fire issued forth, and the land began to sink into the sea. They navigated to the main land in seven large canoes and formed seven traveling groups to insure survival.

These travel groups were the seven sacred clans. This was the beginning of the Cherokee journey toward the cold [north]. The story tells of crossing fertile lands where some stayed and built cities and spoke the ancient language—and hot sand where there was little water—and of crossing four great rivers.

If one traces the journey on a map, the story fits with the four rivers being the Rio Grande, the Red River, the Arkansas, and finally, the Mississippi.

The story tells of the Cherokees encountering other people who were mound builders and sacrificed captives, who they named the "fierce people". Research data suggests that the Cherokees encountered the powerful Iroquois Nation, probably the fierce people referred to, who turned them to the east.

This journey, that had lasted many centuries, finally ended in the direction from where the sun comes up—east—to the mountains that were high, with plenty of water and game and horses, and materials for baskets, pottery, blowguns, and canoes. Here the remaining ones from the original groups lived until the people from across the water that was undrinkable found them. Over their journey, they had built cities and raised crops, and lost, at some point, the ancient language. XLV, XLVI

This story seems to present a realistic understanding of Cherokee origin, particularly when one reviews recent information found by anthropologists, that are similarities between the Cherokee language and the languages of the South Pacific Island people.

This information and the recent findings of the ability of the Pacific Islanders to navigate the Pacific Ocean islands all the way to the American continent, seems to fit well with the Cherokee origin story. The speculation that the Iroquois people turned the Cherokee to the east may well account for the encounter with the fierce people described in the story. The sad part of this journey did not occur until 1830, when the U. S. government passed the "Removal Act", forcing the Cherokees, and other eastern tribes, to leave their homelands and move west.

A review of the historical data, I believe, supports the Cherokee story presented above, and suggests the theory of a group splitting from the Iroquois Nation is simply incomplete, and does not account for the pre-historic origin of the Cherokee Nation.

Chapter 9 - Cherokee Spirituality

Finally, it is important to understand a little about the traditional religious beliefs of the Cherokee people. Although our indigenous people have not been recognized as having a religion, they were a very spiritual people with a strong belief in the Great Creator, God. Prayer was an important part of daily life and ceremonial events. The drum, used in celebration, represents the heart beat of Mother Earth, and each dance has special spiritual meaning.

The traditional religious dance of the Cherokee is the Stomp Dance, held at a sacred site. The Sacred Fire is an eternal flame which is built by the fire keeper and his assistant. They begin at dawn, stoking the burning embers into a large fire for the dance. Seven arbors are located around the fire and dance area. They are made from large poles with brush for the roofs. Each arbor is reserved for one of the seven clans.

The dance cannot begin until each clan is represented. The women prepare a meal for the day. A-ne-jo-di, [Stickball] is played in the afternoon. At sundown, the sermons begin.

The Chief brings out the traditional pipe and fills it with tobacco. The pipe is like a portable altar with the rising smoke being symbolic of one's voice rising to the Creator. The Chief lights the pipe with coals from the sacred fire and takes seven puffs. The Medicine Man from each clan, beginning with the Wolf Clan, takes seven puffs and passes it on. The chief, medicine men and elders then hold a meeting and issue a call for the dance.

The first dance is by invitation and only includes tribal elders, medicine men, and clan heads. The Tribal members then gather to visit and dance until sunrise.

All sacred grounds are posted, requesting no rowdiness, liquor, and the request for general respect.

A series of wampum belts serve to record and read the traditional beliefs and stories. The wampum belts are shown only on very sacred occasions.

Each individual ground has its own schedule for the dances, which is a holy place to worship God, The Creator. Stomp Dance participants include a leader, assistants, and one or more female shell shakers, who wear leg rattles traditionally made from turtle shells filled with pebbles. The shakers provide rhythmic accompaniment while dancing around the fire. The dance cannot begin without the shakers.

The fire is very sacred to traditional Cherokees. It is built at the bottom of a pit below ground.

It is believed that soon after the creation of the Cherokee people, the Creator left his throne in Heaven and visited the earth. He chose four Cherokee men who were strong, healthy, good, and true, and believed with all their heart in the Creator. They were each given a name: Red, Blue, Black, and Yellow. Each was given a wooden stick that was very straight, and told to place one end of the stick on a surface that would not burn, and to place the other end in their hands and start this material that would not burn to magically burn—by giving the sticks a circular rotating motion.

When this was done, they were told to go to the center of the cross, and there the four would start a singular fire. This fire was started with the instructions and help of the Creator. The Sacred Fire has been held since that time by the Cherokee, and kept alive by the Chief Fire-Keeper, and Assistant Fire-Keeper of the Ground. xlvii

In 2010, the U. S. Census Bureau registered 315,000 Cherokee members in the United States. Although some have chosen to worship through other religious denominations, many continue to worship at regular Stomp Dances, and are members of one of the several Sacred Grounds.

My journey has taken almost five years, but the rewards far outweigh the required research and study. It is more than just a family tree, it's the story of my family, and the union of two different cultures through a marriage in the early 1600s. The story demonstrates that we are all children of God, the Creator, and we share far more similarities than differences.

It is my hope that this story might help develop a better under-standing of the path to a more sharing relationship between our two societies in the future.

My efforts have developed an understanding, appreciation and sense of pride beyond anything I could have hoped for! This story brought tears on many occasions, as I studied the tragic way our Native American people were forced from their once proud heritage, to a life of suffering and sacrifice.

As I review my journey, I am reminded of an old Native American proverb that describes my effort: "The soul would have no rainbow if the eye had no tears."

di tsa la gi Sidanelvhi Atlvquodv

~~

Cherokee Family Pride

Appendix A

MEMORIAL

OF

A DELEGATION FROM THE CHEROKEE INDIANS.

———

JANUARY 18, 1831.

Read, and referred to the Committee on Indian Affairs.

———

To the Honorable Senate and House of Representatives of the United States of America in Congress assembled:

The memorial of the undersigned delegation from the Cherokee nation east of the Mississippi, thereto especially instructed by their nation, respectfully showeth unto your honorable bodies the afflictive grievances which it has been their unhappy fate to endure for some time past.

They would respectfully call your attention to the memorials submitted before you during the last session of Congress, embracing subjects of great importance to the interests and welfare of their people, some of which they beg leave at this time again to repeat.

The State of Georgia, in its earnest desire to acquire the extent of her chartered limits, set forth a claim to a large portion of Cherokee lands, as having been purchased under the treaty of the *Indian Springs*, made with the *Creek nation*, and which, it is well known, was rendered null and void by a subsequent treaty, entered into in 1826, in this city, with the same nation. Under the authority of said State, a line has been run by commissioners, comprehending more than a million of acres of land, lying north of the established boundary between the Cherokee and Creek nations, and to which the latter disavowed any pretension of right, claim, or interest. The subject was brought before the President of the United States, who has caused a *third* line to be established, never contended for by any of the parties, and unauthorized by any existing treaty with either nation, though officially declared *shall be* the line between the lands ceded by the Creeks in 1826 to the United States and the Cherokees. On the portion of territory we have thus been deprived of, were the houses and homes of many Cherokees, who have been compelled to leave them, with the farms that afforded their families subsistence. "The tract of land," says Governor Gilmer, in his late message, "from which the Cherokees *have been removed by order of the President*, is supposed to contain 464,646 acres, and *now* subject to be disposed of," &c. From the decision of the President on this subject of boundary, your memorialists, in behalf of their nation, beg leave to appeal, and to question the legal and constitutional powers of the Chief Ma-

b

gistrate to change or alter, in any manner, the established line between the Cherokees and Creeks, without their consent. A difference of opinion had arisen in 1801, between the same nations, relative to a certain part of their boundary; and when the subject was introduced at the War Department by a deputation of Cherokee chiefs, and the interference of the Government solicited, the following reply was given by direction of President Jefferson: "It will be very difficult for the President to ascertain the lines between the several countries of the red people. *They must settle all such contro-versies among themselves. If you cannot agree, how shall we be able to decide correctly?*" [See Minutes of Conferences holden at the War Office, between the Secretary for the Department of War, on behalf of the United States, and a deputation from the Cherokee nation of Indians, on behalf of the said nation, on the 30th of June and 3d of July, 1801.] During the administration of the same eminent lawyer and statesman, the treaty of 1805 was made with the Cherokees, by the third article of which, the right of In-dian nations is admitted, to settle and determine questions of boundary among themselves, viz: "It is also agreed on the part of the United States, that the Government thereof will use its influence and best *endeavors* to *prevail* on the Chickasaw nation of Indians to agree to the following boun-dary between that nation and the Cherokees." &c. "*But it is understood by the contracting parties, that the United States do not engage to have the aforesaid boundary established, but only to prevail on the Chickasaw nation to consent to such a boundary between the two nations.*" By these references, we believe the position of our nation to be fully and clearly sustained; and that its agreement with the Creek nation in 1821, on this subject, is binding to all intents and purposes: and that the sanction of this Government was not essential thereto, to make it so; and that they *alone*, by *voluntary surrender* of their lands, have the right to alter that boundary.

By the treaty made with the Arkansas Cherokees in 1828, inducements were held out to the individuals of our nation to remove west of the Mis-sissippi, and join their brethren, who had withdrawn from their connexion with us in 1817 and 1819, and established for themselves a separate and distinct government, thereby absolving all the political relationship which had previously existed as citizens of the same community. That treaty was never presented to the authority of our nation for its assent, nor the right of the Arkansas Cherokees ever admitted to interfere with, or affect in any manner, the rights and the interests of our people. Under its provi-sions, however, individuals have been induced to emigrate; and in pursu-ance of the stipulation contained in one of the articles, that the Government would make to every individual so emigrating "a just compensation for the property he may abandon," appraisers were appointed by the President, who has extended the term "*property abandoned*" to embrace the houses, farms, and lands upon which situated, *claimed* by emigrants, and who have valued, agreeably to instructions, the improvements so claimed or oc-cupied by them; and it is now contended that the United States have ac-quired a title to the lands as well as to the improvements valued, and per-mission given by the Executive to citizens of the United States to enter the nation, and occupy them to the exclusion of the natives. The lands are, it is well known, not held in severalty by the Cherokees, but *as a nation*; and this right has been solemnly *guarantied* to them by treaty with the United States. The right of *individuals* to cede or transfer any portion of their territory has never been admitted, either by themselves or the Government, and in point of justice and law, all such citizens of the United States who have thus been permitted to enter and settle upon our territory, are intruders, and the faith of this Government is plenged for their removal. We protest against the right of the Arkansas Cherokees, or the Government, to enter into any arrangement to affect our rights contrary to the will of the nation, and also against the introduction and continuance of a population in our country so detrimental to the interests and peace of our citizens, the security of their persons and property from insults and outrage, and as utterly at variance with the plighted faith of this Government, for our territorial protection and promise of good neighbourhood.

It is further contended by the Executive, that the United States have acquired a title to *lands within* the present acknowledged bounds of the nation under the 7th article of the treaty of 1817 with the Cherokees, which stipulated that the United States should lease *to the Indians* improvements that had been abandoned by emigrants, and who had received compensation for the benefit of "the poor and decrepid warriors" of the nation, and which was to be continued until such improvements were "surrendered by the nation or to the nation." By the treaty of 1819, the leases under that of 1817 were declared void, which is of itself sufficient evidence of a surrender *to the nation* of all such improvements as fell within its limits agreeably to the boundary *then* established; and it is moreover declared, that the treaty of 1819 is *a final adjustment of the treaty of* 1817, and the lands then ceded to the United States are *in full satisfaction of all claims* which the United States have on that nation on account of a cession of lands on the Arkansas, for the benefit of the emigrating Cherokees; yet a claim has been asserted by the Executive, on the part of the United States, to a title to lands within our present bounds, acquired under an article in the treaty of 1817, which, by the treaty of 1819, was rendered void, and *fully satisfied*, which, it is said, *enures to the benefit of Georgia*, and is made another plea to allow intrusions. Added to all these are many other intruders, who, without any other pretext than to trespass upon our possessions and our rights, contrary to existing laws, are allowed to annoy and harass our peaceable citizens to an almost insufferable degree. In many instances have they by violence forced the natives out of their houses, and taken possession; while others, less daring, have erected buildings for their own use upon the premises of the objects of their oppression. The frequent complaints made through the agent, and otherwise, to the Government, failed to produce the desired relief from circumstances so well calculated to produce excitement and disturbance between the whites and the red people. To such an alarming extent had intrusion been indulged, that the authority of the nation, relying on an article of treaty, and the former advice of the present Chief Magistrate of the United States when a general of the southern division of the U. S. army, removed a few families who had penetrated far into the country, and of the most exceptionable character—a measure demanded by the security of the persons and property of the Cherokees. It was seized upon and declared a hostile movement, and an armed band of intruders, in retaliation, wreaked their vengeance upon a few peaceable individuals. One was cruelly murdered, another wounded, and a third led a prisoner into Georgia, and thrown into jail, whence he was subsequently released, after much trouble, by a writ of *habeas corpus*. A report of these transactions was made to the Government by the United States' Agent, which, however, resulted only in calling forth language of exception against our chiefs; and the perpetrators of the murder are still trespassing, in open day, upon our rights and our territory, which has drank the blood of an innocent victim to their outrages. During the past summer, the United States' troops were ordered into the nation, as we believe, for the purpose of redeeming the pledges of the Government for our protection; they removed the intruders, who had flocked in thousands to our gold mines, and a few also along the frontier settlements; many, however, were not molested, and others returned in a short time after, placing at utter defiance the authority vested in the United States' Agent, and heretofore exercised by his predecessors. All the Cherokees who had been engaged at their gold mines were removed with the intruders, and experienced much injury and inconvenience under an *order* from the Department of War, and, during the stay of the troops in the nation, were not permitted to re-engage at their mining operations. The troops have been suddenly withdrawn, and our country again left exposed to the ravages of intruders. An act has recently been passed by the Legislature of the State of Georgia, authorizing the Governor thereof to take possession of our gold mines, and appropriating twenty thousand dollars for that purpose; and another providing for the survey of our country into sections, and for the appointment of magistrates therein; against which we would most solemnly protest, as a departure from the obligations of good faith, and the desire to secure and promote the peace and friendship so often repeated in our treaties. The language of the great and illustrious Jefferson, through the Secretary of War, to our chiefs, seems to our memory with peculiar force: "The President listens *willingly* to your representations, and requests you and your nation to be *assured of the friendship of the United States*, and that *all our proceedings* towards you shall be directed by *justice* and a *sacred regard to our treaties*. You must be sensible that the white people are very numerous, and that we should therefore be desirous to buy your land when you are *willing to spare it*, but we *never* wish to buy except when you are *perfectly willing* to sell. The lands we have heretofore bought of you have been marked off by a line, and all beyond that line we consider *absolutely* belonging to our *red brethren*. You shall now receive the map of the last line, which has heretofore been promised to you, to stand in evidence between your people and ours, and to show which lands *belong to you* and which to *us*." (See document before referred to.) We would most earnestly pray that the kind assurances of the friendship of the United States, by one whose examples are so worthy of imitation, may never be passed over with an unfeeling heart for the unfortunate Cherokees; and that all proceedings towards them may be directed by justice and a sacred regard to treaties.

The Executive of the United States, during the past summer, issued an *order* to the agent for our nation, changing the mode of paying the annuity, and providing for its *distribution* amongst the individuals, averaging about forty-two cents to each, contrary to the well known wishes of the Cherokees, and their solemn protest against the measure, the stipulations of existing treaties, and the uniform practice of the Government, down to the payment of the last annuity in 1830. It is a stipend due to the *nation*, and has ever been controlled by its authority. The Cherokees have a treasury, into which it is placed for the support of their Government—"a Government of regular law," modelled agreeably to and in pursuance of the kind and parental advice of President Jefferson, contained in a written address to the Cherokees, 9th of January, 1809—and other national objects, by which means all are enabled to enjoy, in some degree, the benefits arising from its application; but of what possible advantage will it be if paid as contemplated, when hundreds will have a hundred or more miles to travel, neglecting all other business, to obtain the small sum of about forty-two cents? But it cannot be: we protest against any alteration, and humbly hope that you will direct the payment as heretofore, and in conformity with the treaties under which the fund is stipulated. We are aware that it has been asserted that the *chiefs* and others speculate upon this fund, *but it is not so;* even if it were, would it justify a departure from the course which the pledges of the United States have bound its officers to pursue? The language of one so truly the friend of the weak and the oppressed as the Chief Magistrate of the United States in 1808, is too explicit to pass unnoticed on this occasion. To the chiefs of the upper Cherokee towns he spoke as follows: " You *complain* that you do not receive your just proportion of the annuities we pay your *nation*—that the chiefs of the lower towns take for them more than their share. My children, this distribution is made *by the authority of the Cherokee nation,* and according to their *own* rules, over *which we have no control.* We do our *duty* in delivering the annuities to the *head men* of the *nation, and we pretend to no authority over them, to no right of directing how they are to be distributed.'* (See address, signed Th. Jefferson, to the upper Cherokees, dated 4th May, 1808.) That the same mode may still be continued is all we ask, and it is anxiously desired by the whole nation. Since that year there have been "no complaints" on the subject; why then, at this late period, when civilization has taught better the manner in which this small sum should be applied, is the change in the mode of payment to be made?

During the last session of Congress, a bill was passed, whose object, as we understood, was to enable the President of the United States to comply with the compact of 1802, between the United States and the State of Georgia, and afford means to the Indian tribes whose great desires were represented, by the advocates of its passage, to effect their removal west of the Mississippi. It is not desirable for us to remonstrate upon this occasion, but we hope that the kind indulgence of your honorable bodies will be extended while we state some of the many cases of affliction and oppression which have occurred since the passage of the act. A ray of hope, in the midst great apprehension, seemed to shed its glimmering light on the minds of the Cherokees, to learn from the speeches of the Georgia delegation and others, in Congress, that nothing should be practised on the Indians in the operation of the bill, or in connexion with it, that benevolence and humanity could censure; that neither force nor injustice was contemplated by the Government or the authorities of Georgia; and that they should be left to the exercise of their own free will. But experience has taught us to know that a powerful auxiliary has been afforded to forward the views and the policy of that and other States, and of the Executive of the United States, towards the unfortunate aborigines of this continent. They have looked back upon the scenes and prospects of other days, and the contrast with those of the present time has caused much sorrowful feeling. Georgia, in the recent measures put in force to compel the Cherokees to listen and yield to the eloquence of the Secretary of War, and Government's special agent, has departed from the high and magnanimous pledges of kind dealing toward the Indians on the floor of Congress, and has frowned and threatened to prostrate their innocent determination to abide on their ancestral territory;

f

but without effect. She has sent armed guards of fifties, thirties, and tens, in time of profound peace, under pretence of executing her laws, and when the occasion did not require a display of "the pomp and circumstance of war." Leaving the Indian children in destitution, to mourn their hapless lot, she has led their fathers in captivity to a distant land, to destroy their spirits by immuring them in the walls of her prisons. In one case, a white man who had a long while ago taken the protection of the nation, and married a Cherokee woman, and, under the care of the Cherokee nation, had acquired property and a large family, whose interests are identified with those of the Indians, having entered into a mercantile partnership with two Cherokees, he soon fell out with them, and instituted suit against them before the courts of the nation, which decided against him. After this he filed a bill in the Superior Court of Gwinnett county, in Georgia, against the two Cherokees, and prayed a writ of ne exeat, before Augustin S. Clayton, judge of the court, sitting in chancery, who awarded the writ, which was served upon one of them in the Cherokee nation, by a deputy sheriff of Georgia, and under guard of three men, he was carried about eighty miles to the common jail of Gwinnett county, in the said State, where he was kept in close confinement until the sitting of the court in September last, when he was brought up for trial before his honor A. S. Clayton, who issued the writ, and was discharged on the ground that the affidavit of the plaintiff was not sufficient to have warranted the issuing of such a writ. During the same trip by the deputy sheriff, he arrested an elderly Cherokee woman, a married lady with a large family, on a plea of debt, and carried her off captive from her husband and children, fifteen miles on towards Georgia, when she fortunately succeeded in obtaining her liberty by giving bail.

In another case, in the name and authority of George R. Gilmer, Governor of Georgia, a bill was filed in chancery, in the Superior Court of Hall county, in July last, against certain sundry Cherokees, praying for an injunction to stop them from digging and searching for gold within the limits of their own nation; and the bill being sworn to before the same A. S. Clayton, he awarded an injunction against the parties named in the bill as defendants, commanding them, forthwith, to desist from working on those mines, under the penalty of 20,000 dollars, at a time and place where there were unmolested several thousand intruders from Georgia and other States, engaged in robbing the nation of gold, for which the owners were ordered not to work by the said writ. Under the authority of this injunction, the sheriff of Hall county, with an armed force, invaded the nation, consisting of a Colonel, a Captain, and thirty or forty militia of the State of Georgia, who arrested a number of Cherokees engaged in digging for gold, who were at first rescued by the troops of the United States stationed near the place, and the sheriff and his party themselves made prisoners, and conducted fifteen miles to the military camp, when a council of examination was held, and the exhibition of their respective authorities was made, which resulted in the release of the sheriff and his party, and a written order by the commanding officer of the United States troops, directing the Cherokees to submit to the authority of Georgia, and that no further protection could be extended to the Cherokees at the gold mines, as he could no longer interfere with the laws of Georgia, but would afford aid in carrying them into execution. On the return of the sheriff and his party, they passed by the Cherokees, who were still engaged in digging for gold, and ordered them to desist, under the penalty of being committed to jail, and proceeded to destroy their tools and machinery for gleaning gold, and after committing some further aggression, they returned. Shortly afterwards, the sheriff, with a guard of four men, and a process from the State of Georgia, arrested three Cherokees for disobeying the injunction, while peaceably engaged in their labors, and conducted them to Watkinsville, a distance of seventy-five miles, before the same A. S. Clayton, who then and there sentenced them to pay a fine of ninety-three dollars, cost, and stand committed to prison until paid, and also compelled them to give their bond in the sum of one thousand dollars, for their personal appearance before his next court, to answer the charges of violating the writ of injunction aforesaid. In custody they were retained five days, paid the cost, gave the required bond, and did appear accordingly, as bound by Judge Clayton, who dismissed them on the ground that the Governor of Georgia, could not become a prosecutor in the case. For the unwarrantable outrage committed on their liberty and persons, no apology was made, and the cost they had paid was not refunded.

During the past summer, a Cherokee was arrested in the nation by an officer of the State of Georgia on a charge for murder committed upon the body of another Indian, in said nation, and carried to Hall county, and placed in jail, to await his trial under the laws of that State. After some months confinement, he was taken out, and tried by the aforesaid A. S. Clayton, and sentenced by him to be executed on the 24th December last. An application was made to the Chief Justice of the United States for a writ of error, in order that the case might be brought before the Supreme Court of the United States, to test the constitutionality of the proceedings, and was obtained. The arbitrary manner in which the citation was treated by the Governor and Legislature, then in session, are known to you. The resolutions adopted on the occasion breathe a spirit towards our nation of which we will not permit ourselves to speak: suffice it to say, therefore, that the writ of error has been disregarded, and the unfortunate man executed agreeably to the sentence of the Judge.

One other case: A party of armed men, ten in number, from De Kalb county, Georgia, committed numerous outrages, under the pretence of being Georgia officers, as far as seventy-five miles within the nation. They arrested a Cherokee without cause, and compelled him to pay a horse for his release. Under forged claims, they attempted to arrest another individual, and, with him, his negroes, but failed: arrived at the residence of another, in his absence, they were in the act of driving his cattle off, when they were rescued by his neighbors, though they succeeded in committing some robbery upon the house. At another place they turned from an Indian his horse, without even a pretended claim, and cruelly abused the persons of two aged Cherokees, one a female, causing a flow of blood, because they did not quietly suffer themselves to be robbed of their property. Two of their children, who had felt it their duty to interfere for the protection of their aged parents from an insult and outrage so barbarous, were led captive into Georgia, and compelled for their liberty to give their notes for one hundred dollars, each, payable in ten days!!!

Many other cases of aggravating character could be stated, did the nature of a memorial allow, supported by unexceptionable evidence. To convince the United States of our friendship and devotedness to treaty obligations, we have endured much, though with bleeding hearts, but in peace. And we hope enough has been done to convince even the most sceptic that a treaty "on reasonable terms" can never be obtained of our nation, and that it is

h

time to close this scene of operations, never contemplated by the compact between the State of Georgia and the United States. How far we have been able to keep bright the chain of friendship which binds us to these United States, is within the reach of your knowledge. It is ours to maintain it, until, perhaps, the plaintive voice of an Indian from the south shall no more be heard within your halls of legislation. Our nation and our people may cease to exist before another revolving year re-assembles this august assembly of great men. We implore that our people may not be denounced as savages, unfit for the "good neighborhood" guaranteed to them by treaty. We cannot better express the rights of our nation than they are developed on the face of the document we herewith submit; and the desires of our nation, than to pray a faithful fulfilment of the promises made by its illustrious author through his Secretary. Between the compulsive measures of Georgia and our destruction we ask the interposition of your authority, and a remembrance of the bond of perpetual peace pledged for our safety, the safety of the last fragments of once mighty nations, that have gazed for a while upon your civilization and prosperity, but which now totter on the brink of angry billows, whose waves have covered in oblivion other nations that were once happy, but are now no more!

The schools where our children learn to read the word of God, the churches where our people now sing to his praise, and where they are taught that "of one blood he created all the nations of the earth;" the fields they have cleared, and the orchards they have planted; the houses they built, are all dear to the Cherokees, and there they expect to live and to die, on the lands inherited from their fathers, as the firm friends of all the people of these United States.

R. TAYLOR,
JOHN RIDGE,
W. S. COODEY,
In behalf of the Cherokee Nation.

Washington City, 15th January, 1831.

To the beloved Chief of the Cherokee nation, the Little Turkey, on behalf of the said nation, the Secretary of War of the United States sends greeting:

Friend and Brother: The deputation appointed by you to visit the seat of Government have arrived, and been welcomed by your father, the President of the United States, with cordiality; they have spoken, and he has heard all the representations that they were instructed by you, on behalf of the Cherokee nation, to make to him. In his name, I have answered them in sincerity and truth; and when they shall report to you what I have said, I trust that you will feel all uneasiness removed from your minds, and that you and your nation will experience that satisfaction which must result from a conviction of the certainty with which you may continue to rely on the protection and friendship of the United States.

These can never be forfeited but by the misconduct of the red people themselves. Your father, the President, instructs me to assure you, in behalf of your nation, that he will pay the most sacred regard to the existing treaties between your nation and ours, and protect your whole territory against all intrusions that may be attempted by white people; that all en-

ouragement shall be given to you in your just pursuits and laudable progress towards comfort and happiness, by the introduction of useful arts; that
all persons who shall offend against our treaties, or against the laws made for
your protection, shall be brought to justice, or, if this should be impracticable, that a faithful remuneration shall be made to you; and that he will never
abandon his beloved Cherokees nor their children, so long as they shall act
justly and peaceably towards the white people and their red brethren.

This is all that he requires from you in return for his friendship and protection: he trusts you will not force him to recede from these determinations by an improper and unjust change of conduct, but that you will give
him abundant reason to increase, if possible, his desire to see you happy and
contented under the fostering care of the United States.

I send you by your beloved chief, The Glass, a chain; it is made of gold,
which will never rust; and I pray the Great Spirit to assist us in keeping
the chain of our friendship, of which this golden chain is meant as an emblem,
bright for a long succession of ages.

H. DEARBORN, *Secretary of War.*

WAR DEPARTMENT, *7th July,* 1801.

[Because the previous pages are so hard to read in this book, please allow me to type up what they say, as I feel they are very important.]

MEMORIAL

OF

A DELEGATION FROM THE CHEROKEE INDIANS

—<>—

January 18, 1831

Read, and referred to the Committee on Indian Affairs

—<>—

To the Honorable Senate and House of Representatives of the United States of America in Congress assembled:

The memorial of the undersigned delegation from the Cherokee nation east of the Mississippi, thereto especially instructed by their nation, respectfully showeth unto your honorable bodies the afflictive grievances which it has been their unhappy fate to endure for some time past.

k

They would respectfully call your attention to the memorials submitted before you during the last session of Congress, embracing subjects of great importance to the interests and welfare of their people, some of which they beg leave at this time again to repeat.

The State of Georgia, in its earnest desire to acquire the extent of her chartered limits, set forth a claim to a large portion of Cherokee lands, as having been purchased under the treaty of the Indian Springs, made with the Creek nation, and which, it is well know, was rendered null and void by a subsequent treaty, entered into in 1826, in this city, with the same nation. Under the authority of said State, a line has been run by commissioners, comprehending more than a million of acres of land, lying north of the established boundary between the Cherokee and Creek nations, and to which the latter disavowed any pretension of right, claim, or interest. The subject was brought before the President of the United States, who has caused a *third* line to be established, never contended for by any of the parties, and unauthorized by any existing treaty with either nation, though officially declared *shall be* the line between the lands ceded by the Creeks in 1826 to the United States and the Cherokees. On the portion of territory we have thus been deprived of, were the houses and homes of many Cherokees, who have been compelled to leave them, with the farms that afforded their families subsistence. "The tract of land," says Governor Gilmer, in his late message, "from which the Cherokees *have been removed by order of the President,* is supposed to contain 464,646 acres, and *now* subject to be disposed of," &c. From the decision of the President on this subject of boundary, your memorialists, in behalf of their nation, beg leave to appeal, and to question the legal and constitutional powers of the Chief Magistrate to change or alter, in any manner, the established

1

line between the Cherokees and Creeks, without their consent. A difference of opinion had arisen in 1801, between the same nations, relative to a certain part of their boundary; and when the subject was introduced at the War Department by a deputation of Cherokee chiefs, and the interference of the Government solicited, the following reply was given by direction of President Jefferson: "It will be very difficult for the President to ascertain the lines between the several countries of the red people. *They must settle all such controversies among themselves. If you cannot agree, how shall we be able to decide correctly?*" [See Minutes of Conferences holden at the War Office, between the secretary for the Department of War, on behalf of the United States, and a deputation from the Cherokee nation of Indians, on behalf of the said nation, on the 30th of June and 3d of July, 1801.] During the administration of the same eminent lawyer and statesman, the treaty of 1806 was made with the Cherokees, by the third article of which, the right of Indian nations is admitted, to settle and determine questions of boundary among themselves, viz: "It is also agreed on the part of the United States, that the Government thereof will use its influence and best endeavors to *prevail* on the Chickasaw nation of Indians to agree to the following boundary between that nation and the Cherokees," &c. "*But it is understood by the contracting parties, that the United States do not engage to have the aforesaid boundary established, but only to prevail on the Chickasaw nation to consent to such a boundary between the two nations.*" By these references, we believe the position of our nation to be fully and clearly sustained; and that its agreement with the Creek nation in 1821, on this subject, is biding to all intents and purposes; and that the sanction of this Government was not essential thereto, to make it so; and that they

m

alone, by *voluntary surrender* of their lands, have the right to alter that boundary.

By the treaty made with the Arkansas Cherokees in 1828, inducements were held out to the individuals of our nation to remove west of the Mississippi, and join their brethren, who had withdrawn from their connexion with us in 1816 and 1819, and established for themselves a separate and distinct government, thereby absolving all the political relationship which had previously existed as citizens of the same community. That treaty was never presented to the authority of our nation for its assent, nor the right of the Arkansas Cherokees ever admitted to interfere with, or affect in any manner, the rights and the interests of our people. Under its provisions, however, individuals have been induced to emigrate; and in pursuance of the stipulation contained in one of the articles, that the Government would make to every individual so emigrating "a just compensation for the property he may abandon," appraisers were appointed by the President, who has extended the term *"property abandoned"* to embrace the houses, farms, and lands upon which situated, *claimed* by emigrants, and who have valued, agreeably to instructions, the improvements so claimed or occupied by them; and it is now contended that the United States have acquired a title to the lands as well as to the improvements valued, and permission given by the Executive to citizens of the United States to enter the nation, and occupy them to the exclusion of the natives. The lands are, it is well known, not held in severalty by the Cherokees, but *as a nation*; and this right has been solemnly *guarantied* to them by treaty with the United States. The right of *individuals* to cede or transfer any portion of their territory has never been admitted, either by themselves or the Government; and in point of justice and law, all such citizens of the United States who have thus been permitted to enter and settle upon our territory, are intruders, and the faith of this Government is pledged for their removal. We protest against the right of the Arkansas Cherokee, or the Government, to enter into any arrangement to effect our rights contrary to the will of the nation, and also against the introduction and continuance of a population in our country so detrimental to the interests and peace of our citizens, the security of their persons and property from insults and outrage, and so utterly at variance with the plighted faith of this Government, for our territorial protection and promise of good neighborhood.

It is further contended by the Executive, that the United States have acquired a title to *lands within* the present acknowledged bounds of the nation under the 7th article of the treaty of 1817 with the Cherokees, which stipulated that the United States should lease *to the Indians* improvements that had been abandoned by emigrants, and who had received compensation for the benefit of "the poor and decrepid warriors" of the nation, and which was to be continued until such improvements were "surrendered by the nation or to the nation." By the treaty of 1819, the leases under that of 1817 were declared void, which is of itself sufficient evidence of a surrender *to the nation* of all such improvements as fell within its limits agreeably to the boundary *then* established; and it is moreover declared, that the treaty of 1819 is a *final adjustment of the treaty of* 1817, and the lands then ceded to the United States are in *full satisfaction of all claims* which the United States have on that nation on account of a cession of lands on the Arkansas, for the benefit of the emigrating Cherokees; yet a claim has been asserted by the Executive, on the part of the United States, to a title to lands within our present bounds, acquired under an article in the treaty of 1817, which, by the treaty of 1819, was rendered void, and *fully satisfied*, which, it is said, *ensures to the benefit of Georgia*, and is made another plea to allow intrusion. Added to all these are many other intruders, who, without any other pretext than to trespass upon our possessions and our rights, contrary to existing laws, are allowed to annoy and harass our peaceable citizens to an almost insufferable degree. In many instances have they by violence forced the natives out of their houses, and taken possession; while others, less daring, have erected buildings for their own use upon the premises of the objects of their oppression. The frequent complaints made through the agent, and otherwise, to the Government, failed to produce the desired relief from circumstances so well calculated to produce excitement and disturbance between the whites and the red people. To such an alarming extent had intrusion been indulged, that the authority of the nation, relying on an article of treaty, and the former advice of the present Chief Magistrate of the United States when a general of the southern division of the U.S. army, removed a few families who had penetrated far into the country, and of the most exceptionable character—a measure demanded by the security of the persons and property of the Cherokees. It was seized upon and declared a hostile movement, and an armed band of intruders, in retaliation, wreaked their vengeance upon a few peaceable individuals. One was cruelly murdered, another wounded, and a third led a prisoner into Georgia, and thrown into jail, whence he was subsequently released, after much trouble, by a writ of *habeas corpus*. A report of these transactions was made to the Government by the United States' Agent, which, however, resulted only in calling forth language of exception against our chiefs; and the perpetrators of the murder are still trespassing, in open day,

p

upon our rights and our territory, which has drank the blood of an innocent victim to their outrages. During the past summer, the United States' troops were ordered into the nation, as we believe, for the purpose of redeeming the pledges of the Government for our protection; they removed the intruders, who had flocked in thousands to our gold mines, and a few also along the frontier settlements; many, however, were not molested, and others returned in a short time after, placing at utter defiance the authority vested in the United States' Agent, and heretofore exercised by his predecessors. All the Cherokees who had been engaged at their gold mines were removed with the intruders, and experienced much injury and inconvenience under an *order* from the Department of War, and, during the stay of the troops in the nation, were not permitted to re-engage at their mining operations. The troops have suddenly withdrawn, and our country again left exposed to the ravages of intruders. An act has recently been passed by the Legislature of the State of Georgia, authorizing the Governor thereof to take possession of our gold mines, and appropriating twenty thousand dollars for that purpose; and another providing for the survey of our country into sections, and for the appointment of magistrates therein; against which we would most solemnly protest, as a departure from the obligations of good faith, and the desire to secure and promote the peace and friendship so often repeated in our treaties. The language of the great and illustrious Jefferson, through the Secretary of War, to our chiefs, recurs to our memory with peculiar force: "The President listens *willingly* to your representations, and requests you and your nation to be *assured of the friendship of the United States*, and that *all our proceedings* towards you shall be directed by *justice* and a *sacred regard to our treaties*. You must be sensible that the white people are very numerous, and that we should therefore be desirous to buy your land when you are *willing* to spare it, but we *never* wish to buy except when you are *perfectly willing* to sell. The lands we have heretofore bought of you have been marked off by a line, and all beyond that line we consider *absolutely* belonging to our *red brethren*. You shall now receive the map of the last line, which has heretofore been promised to you, to stand in evidence between *your* people and *ours*, and to show which lands *belong* to *you* and which to *us*." (See document before referred to.) We would most earnestly pray that the kind assurances of the friendship of the United States, by one whose examples are so worthy of imitation, may never be passed over with an unfeeling heart for the unfortunate Cherokees; and that all proceedings towards them may be directed by justice and a sacred regard to treaties.

The Executive of the United States, during the past summer, issued an *order* to the agent for our nation, changing the mode of paying the annuity, and providing for its *distribution* amongst the individuals, averaging about forty-two cents to each, contrary to the well known wishes of the Cherokees, and their solemn protest against the measure, the stipulations of existing treaties, and the uniform practice of the Government, down to the payment of the last annuity in 1830. It is a stipend due to the *nation*, and has ever been controlled by its authority. The Cherokees have a treasury, into which it is placed for the support of their Government—"a Government of regular law," modelled agreeably to and in pursuance of the kind and parental advice of President Jefferson, contained in a written address to the Cherokees, 9th of January, 1809—and other national objects, by which means all are enabled to enjoy, in some degree, the benefits arising from its application; but of what possible advantage will it be if pain as contemplated, when hundreds will have a hundred or more miles to travel, neglecting all other business, to obtain the small sum of about forty-two cents? But it cannot be: we protest against any alteration, and humbly hope that you will direct the payment as heretofore, and in conformity with the treaties that the *chiefs* and others speculate upon this fund, *but it is not so*; even if it were, would it justify a departure from the course which the pledges of the United States in 1808, is too explicit to pass unnoticed on this occasion. To the Chiefs of the upper Cherokee towns he spoke as follows: "You *complain* that you do not receive your just proportion of the annuities we pay your *nation*---that the chiefs of the lower towns take for them more than their share. My children, this distribution is made *by the authority of the Cherokee nations*, and according to their *own* rules, over *which we have no control*. We do our *duty* in delivering the annuities to the *head men* of the nation, and *we pretend to no authority over them, to no right of directing how they are to be distributed*.' (See address, signed The Jefferson, to the upper Cherokees, dated 4th May, 1808.) That the same mode may still be continued is all we ask, and it is anxiously desired by the whole nation. Since that year there have been "no complaints" on the subject, why then, at this later period, when civilization has taught better the manner in which this small sum should be applied, is the charge in the mode of payment to be made?

During the last session of Congress, a bill was passed, whose object, as we understood, was to enable the President of the United States to comply with the compact of 1802, between the United States and the State of Georgia, and afford means to the Indian tribes whose great desires were represented, by the advocates of its passage, to effect their removal west of the Mississippi. It is not desirable for us to remonstrate upon this occasion, but we hope that the kind indulgence of your honorable bodies will be extended while we state some of the many cases of affection and oppression which have occurred since the passage of the act. A ray of hope, in the midst great apprehension, seemed to shed its glimmering light on the minds of the Cherokees, to learn from the speeches of the Georgia delegation and others, in Congress, that nothing should be practised on the Indians in the operation of the bill, or in connexion with it, that benevolence and humanity could censure; that neither force nor injustice was contemplated by the Government or the authorities of Georgia; and that they should be left to the exercise of their own free will. But experience has taught us to know that a powerful auxiliary has been afforded to forward the views and the policy of that and other States, and of the Executive of the United States, towards the unfortunate aborigines of this continent. They have looked back upon the scenes and prospects of other days, and the contrasts of those of the present time has caused much sorrowful feeling. Georgia, in the recent measures put in force to compel the Cherokees to listen and yield to the eloquence of the Secretary of War, and Government's special agent, has departed from the high and magnanimous pledges of kind dealing toward the Indians on the floor of Congress, and has frowned and threatened to prostrate their innocent determination to abide on their ancestral territory: but without effect. She has sent armed guards of fifties, thirties, and tens, in time of profound peace, under pretence of executing her laws, and when the occasion did not require a display of "the pomp and circumstance of war." Leaving the Indian children in destitution, to mourn their hapless lot, she has led their fathers in captivity to a distant land, to destroy their spirits by immuring them in the walls of her

t

prisons. In one case, a white man who had a long while ago taken the protection of the nation, and married a Cherokee woman, and, under the care of the Cherokee nation, had acquired property and a large family, whose interests are identified with those of the Indians, having entered into a mercantile partnership with two Cherokees, he soon fell out with them, and instituted suit against them before the courts of the nation, which decided against him. After this he filed a bill in the Superior Court of Gwinnett county, in Georgia, against the two Cherokees, and prayed a writ of *ne exeat*, before Augustin S. Clayton, judge of the court, sitting in chancery, who awarded the writ, which was served upon one of them in the Cherokee nation, by a deputy sheriff of Georgia, and under guard of three men, he was carried about eighty miles to the common jail of Gwinnett county, in the said State, where he was kept in close confinement until the sitting of the court in September last, when he was brought up for trial before his honor A. S. Clayton, who issued the writ, and was discharged on the ground that the affidavit of the plaintiff was not sufficient to have warranted the issuing of such a writ. During the same trip by the deputy sheriff, he arrested an elderly Cherokee woman, a married lady with a large family, on a plea of debt, and carried her off captive from her husband and children, fifteen miles on towards Georgia, when she fortunately succeeded in obtaining her liberty by giving bail.

In another case, in the name and authority of George R. Gilmer, Governor of Georgia, a bill was filed in chancery, in the Superior Court of Hall county, in July last, against certain sundry Cherokees, praying for an injunction to stop them from digging and searching for gold within the limits of their own nation; and the bill being sworn to before the same A. S. Clayton, he awarded an injunction against the parties

u

named in the bill as defendants, commanding them, forthwith, to desist from working on those mines, under the penalty of 20,000 dollars, at a time and place where there were unmolested several thousand intruders from Georgia and other States, engaged in robbing the nation of gold, for which the owners were ordered not to work by the said writ. Under the authority of this injunction, the sheriff of Hall county, with an *armed force*, invaded the nation, consisting of a Colonel, a Captain, thirty or forty militia of the State of Georgia, who arrested a number of Cherokees engaged in digging for gold, who were at first rescued by the troops of the United States stationed near the place, and the sheriff and his party themselves made prisoners, and conducted fifteen miles to the military camp, when a council of examination was held, and the exhibition of their respective authorities was made, which resulted in the release of the sheriff and his party, and a written order by the commanding officer of the United States troops, directing the Cherokees to submit to the authority of Georgia, and that no further protection could be extended to the Cherokee at the gold mines, as he could no longer interfere with the laws of Georgia, but would afford aid in carrying them into execution. On the return of the sheriff and his party, they passed by the Cherokees, who were still engaged in digging for gold, and ordered them to desist, under the penalty of being committed to jail, and proceeded to destroy their tools and machinery for gleaning gold, and after committing some further aggression, they returned. Shortly afterwards, the sheriff, with a guard of four men, and a process from the State of Georgia, arrested three Cherokees for disobeying the injunction, while peaceably engaged in their labors, and conducted them to Wadkinsville, a distance of seventy-five miles, before the same A. S. Clayton, who then and there sentenced them to pay a fine of ninety-three dollars, cost, and stand committed to prison until paid, and also compelled them to give their bond in the sum of one thousand dollars, for their personal appearance before his next court, to answer the charges of violating the writ of injunction aforesaid. In custody they were retained five days, paid the cost, gave the required bond, and did appear accordingly, as bound by Judge Clayton, who dismissed them on the ground that the Governor of Georgia, could not become a prosecutor in the case. For the unwarrantable outrage committed on their liberty and persons, no apology was made, and the cost they had paid was not refunded.

During the past summer, a Cherokee was arrested in the nation by an officer of the State of Georgia on a charge for murder committed upon the body of another Indian, in said nation, and carried to Hall county, and placed in jail, to await his trial under the laws of that State. After some months confinement, he was taken out, and tried by the aforesaid A. S. Clayton, and sentenced by him to be executed on the 24th December last. An application was made to the Chief Justice of the United States for a writ of error, in order that the case might be brought before the Supreme Court of the United States, to test the constitutionality of the proceedings, and was obtained. The arbitrary manner in which the citation was treated by the Governor and Legislature, then in session, are known to you. The resolutions adopted on the occasion breathe a spirit towards our nation of which we will not permit ourselves to speak: suffice it to say, therefore, that the writ of error has been disregarded, and the unfortunate man executed agreeably to the sentence of the Judge.

One other case: A party of armed men, ten in number, from De Kalb county, Georgia, committed numerous outrages, under the pretence of being Georgia officers, as far as seventy-five miles within the nation. They arrested a Cherokee without cause, and compelled him to pay a horse for his release. Under forged claims, they attempted to arrest another individual, and, with him, the negroes, but failed: arrived at the residence of another, in his absence, they were in the act of driving his cattle off, when they were rescued by his neighbors, though they succeeded in committing some robbery upon the house. At another place they forced from an Indian his horse, without even a pretended claim, and cruelly abused the persons of two aged Cherokees, one female, causing a flow of blood, because they did not quietly suffer themselves to be robbed of their property. Two of their children, who had felt it their duty to interfere for the protection of their aged parents from an insult and outrage so barbarous, were led captive into Georgia, and compelled for their liberty to give their notes for one hundred dollars, each, payable in ten days!!!

Many other cases of aggravating character could be stated, did the nature of a memorial allow, supported by unexceptionable evidence. To convince the United States of our friendship and devotedness to treaty obligations, we have endured much, though with bleeding hearts, but in peace. And we hope enough has been done to convince even the most sceptic that a treaty "on reasonable terms" can never be obtained of our nation, and that it is time to close this scene of operations, never contemplated by the compact between the State of Georgia and the United States. How far we have contributed to keep bright the chain of friendship which binds us to these United States, is within the reach of your knowledge. It is ours to maintain it, until, perhaps, the plaintive voice of an Indian from the south shall no more be heard within your halls of legislation. Our nation and our people may cease to exist before another revolving year re-assembles this August assembly of great men. We implore that our people may not be denounced as *savages*, unfit for the "good neighborhood" guarantied to them by treaty. We cannot better express the rights of our nation than they are developed on the face of the document we herewith submit; and the desires of our nation, than to pray a faithful fulfilment of the promises made by its illustrious author through his Secretary. Between the compulsive measures of Georgia and our destruction we ask the interposition of your authority, and a remembrance of the bond of perpetual peace pledged for our safety, the safety of the last fragments of once mighty Nations, that have gazed for a while upon your civilization and prosperity, but which now totter on the brink of angry billows, whose waves have covered in oblivion other nations that were once happy, but are now no more!

The schools where our children learn to read the word of God, the churches where our people now sing to his praise, and where they are taught that "of one blood he created all the nations of the earth;" the fields they have cleared, and the orchards they have planted; the houses they have built, are all dear to the Cherokees, and there they expect to live and to die, on the lands inherited from their fathers, as the firm friends of all the people of these United States.

R. TAYLOR,

JOHN RIDGE,

W. S. COODEY,

In behalf of the Cherokee Nation.

Washington City, 15th January, 1831.

———

To the beloved Chief of the Cherokee nation, the Little Turkey, on
behalf of the said nation, the Secretary of War of the United States
sends greeting:

Friend and Brother: The deputation appointed by you to visit the seat
of Government have arrived, and been welcomed by your father, the
President of the United States, with cordiality; they have spoken, and
he has heard all the representations that they were instructed by you, on
behalf of the Cherokee nation, to make to him. In his name, I have
answered them in sincerity and truth; and when they shall report to you
what I have said, I trust that you will feel all uneasiness removed from
your minds, and that you and your nation will experience that
satisfaction which must result from a conviction of the certainty with
which you may continue to rely on the protection and friendship of the
United States.

These can never be forfeited but by the misconduct of the red people
themselves. Your father, the President, instructs me to assure you, in
behalf of your nation, that he will pay the most sacred regard to the
existing treaties between your nation and ours, and protect your whole
territory against all intrusions that may be attempted by white people;
that all encouragement shall be given to you in your just pursuits and
laudable progress towards comfort and happiness, by the introduction
of useful arts; that all persons who shall offend against our treaties, or
against the laws made for your protection, shall be brought to justice,
or, if this should be impracticable, that a faithful remuneration shall be
made to you; and that he will never abandon his beloved Cherokees nor
their children, so long as they shall act justly and peaceably towards the

white people and their red brethren.

This is all that he requires from you in return for his friendship and protection: he trusts you will not force him to recede from these determinations by an improper and unjust change of conduct, but that you will give him abundant reasons to increase, if possible, his desire to see you happy and contented under the fostering care of the United States.

I send you by your beloved chief, The Glass, a chain; it is made of gold, which will never rust; and I pray the Great Spirit to assist us in keeping the chain of our friendship, of which this golden chain is meant as an emblem, bright for a long succession of ages.

H. DEARBORN, Secretary of War.

War Department, 7th July, 1801

Appendix B

1—William Thomas Carpenter (29 October 1549 – 12 October 1622)

+Lady Anne Stroud (1550 – 1623)

..2—Robert Carpenter (1578 – 1 December 1651)

..+Susan Pasmere Jeffery (about 1579 – 1651)

....3—Thomas Pasmere Carpenter (1607 –)

....+Pride "Chalakahatha-Shawnee Woman" Cornstalk (1615 – 1679)

......4—Amatoya "Trader Carpenter" Moytoy I (1635 – 1730)

......+Locha (1640 – about 1692)

........5—Amatoya "Trader Tom Carpenter" Moytoy II (1660 – about 1734)

........+Nancy "Ani'-Ga'tage'wi'" (1664 – about 1732)

..........6—Amatoya "Savannah Tom Carpenter" Moytoy III (abut 1680 – April 1711)

..........+Nancy Tenase "Aniwaya" Moytoy (1683 – about 1741)

..........6—Amatoya "White Owl Raven Carpenter" Moytoy IV (1676 –)

..........+Nancy Tenase "Aniwaya" Moytoy (1683 – about 1741)

...........7—Attacullakulla "Little Carpenter" Carpenter (1699 – 1780-1785)

...........+Nionne "Paint Clan" Ollie (–)

.............8—Dutsi "Dutch" Carpenter (–)

.............+E-LI-SI "Deer Clan" (–)

...............9—Major "Ka-Nun-Tla-Ela-Geh" Ridge (1771 – 22 June 1839)

...............+Suzannah Catherine "Sehoyah" Wickett (–)

.................10—John "Skah-tle-loh-skee" Ridge (1802 – 22 June 1839)

.................+Sarah Bird Northrup (–)

...............9—David "Oo-Wa-Tie" Uwatie (–)

...............+Susanna Reese (–)

.................10—Elias "Gallegina Uwatie, Buck Watie" Boudinot (1802 – 22 June 1839)

.................10—Stand "Degataga, Isaac" Watie (12 December 1806 – 9 September 1871)

...........7—Oosta "White Owl Great Eagle" Carpenter (1723 –)

...........+Alexander Drumgoole (1720 –)

.............8—Alexander Drumgoole, Sr. (about 1750 – about 1824)

.............+Nancy Augusta (about 1756 – after 1828)

...............9—Alexander "WI-HU" Drumgoole, Jr. (1785 – 1847)

...............+I-NO-WA-GA GO-LO-NU-GI "Peggy" (1790 – 1851)

.................10—Sarah Drumgoole (1817 – 1 January 1879)

.................+Samuel Ballard, Sr. (11 April 1800 – 16 March 1863)

...................11—Minerva "Cho-y-u-kah" Ballard (14 October 1841 – 13 July 1913)

...................+George Washington Countryman (30 May 1839 – 19 June 1914)

.....................12—Ann Eliza Countryman (March 1863 – 23 October 1941)

.....................+John L. Courtney (13 March 1850 – 18 April 1920)

.......................13—Minerva Courtney (25 December 1886 – 11 February 1920)

.......................+Otho Miller Story, Sr. (4 April 1880 – 27 April 1966)

.........................14—Otho Miller Story, Jr. (1916 – 2005)

.........................+Floy Mae Bell (1915 – 2014)

...........................15—**Iris Edd Story (1939 –)**

......+QUE-DI-SI "Quatsy" Ani'-wa'ya (1650 – 1692)

........5 — Tame Doe Moytoy (–)

........+Francis "Anakwanki Skayagustowo" Fivekiller (1710 – 1791)

...........6 — Nancy "Nanye-hi" Ward, Beloved Woman of the Cherokees (17 Jul 1736 – 30 Mar 1822)

..........+Bryant Ward (1720 – 15 August 1815)

........5 — Nancy Tenase "Aniwaya" Moytoy (1683 – about 1741)

........+Amatoya "Savannah Tom Carpenter" Moytoy III (about 1680 – April 1711)

........+Amatoya "White Owl Raven Carpenter" Moytoy IV (1676 –)

SEE ABOVE FOR DESCENDANTS OF Nancy Tenase "Aniwaya" Moytoy

........5 — Kanagatoga "Old Hop Standing Turkey Carpenter" Moytoy (1690 – August 1761)

........+SU-GI "Wild Onion Rainmaker" (1692 – 1735)

...........6 — Granny Hopper "Grasshopper" Carpenter (1730 – 1785)

..........+James William David McDaniel, Sr. (1721 – 1782)

...........7 — Catherine McDaniel (1763 – 1822)

...........+John "Jack" Ward (1755 – 1815)

..............8 — George M. "UG-TI-GA" Ward (17 March 1787 – 1863)

..............+Mary Kinchlov (–)

................9 — Martha "Patsy" Ward (22 February 1819 – 1859)

................+John Countryman (1810-1814 – about 1862)

.................10 — George Washington Countryman (30 May 1839 – 19 June 1914)

.................+Minerva "Cho-y-u-kah" Ballard (14 October 1841 – 13 July 1913)

SEE ABOVE FOR DESCENDANTS OF George Washington Countryman

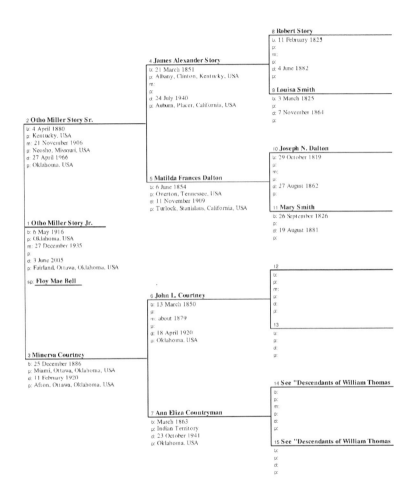

8 Robert Story
b: 11 February 1825
p:
m:
p:
d: 4 June 1882
p:

9 Louisa Smith
b: 3 March 1825
p:
d: 7 November 1864
p:

4 James Alexander Story
b: 21 March 1851
p: Albany, Clinton, Kentucky, USA
m:
p:
d: 24 July 1940
p: Auburn, Placer, California, USA

10 Joseph N. Dalton
b: 29 October 1819
p:
m:
p:
d: 27 August 1862
p:

11 Mary Smith
b: 26 September 1826
p:
d: 19 August 1881
p:

2 Otho Miller Story Sr.
b: 4 April 1880
p: Kentucky, USA
m: 21 November 1906
p: Neosho, Missouri, USA
d: 27 April 1966
p: Oklahoma, USA

5 Matilda Frances Dalton
b: 6 June 1854
p: Overton, Tennessee, USA
d: 11 November 1909
p: Turlock, Stanislaus, California, USA

1 Otho Miller Story Jr.
b: 6 May 1916
p: Oklahoma, USA
m: 27 December 1935
p:
d: 3 June 2005
p: Fairland, Ottawa, Oklahoma, USA

sp: **Floy Mae Bell**

12
b:
p:
m:
p:
d:
p:

13
b:
p:
d:
p:

6 John L. Courtney
b: 13 March 1850
p:
m: about 1879
p:
d: 18 April 1920
p: Oklahoma, USA

3 Minerva Courtney
b: 25 December 1886
p: Miami, Ottawa, Oklahoma, USA
d: 11 February 1920
p: Afton, Ottawa, Oklahoma, USA

14 See "Descendants of William Thomas
b:
p:
m:
p:
d:
p:

7 Ann Eliza Countryman
b: March 1863
p: Indian Territory
d: 23 October 1941
p: Oklahoma, USA

15 See "Descendants of William Thomas
b:
p:
d:
p:

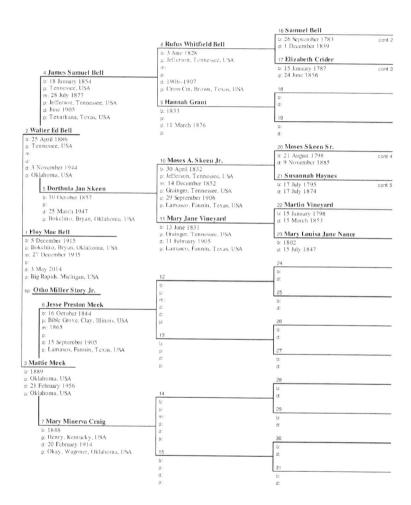

16 Samuel Bell
b: 26 September 1783   cont 2
d: 1 December 1839

17 Elizabeth Crider
b: 15 January 1787   cont 3
d: 24 June 1856

18
b:
d:

19
b:
d:

8 Rufus Whitfield Bell
b: 3 June 1828
p: Jefferson, Tennessee, USA
m:
p:
d: 1906–1907
p: Cross Cut, Brown, Texas, USA

9 Hannah Grant
b: 1833
p:
d: 11 March 1876
p:

4 James Samuel Bell
b: 18 January 1854
p: Tennessee, USA
m: 28 July 1877
p: Jefferson, Tennessee, USA
d: June 1905
p: Texarkana, Texas, USA

20 Moses Skeen Sr.
b: 21 August 1798   cont 4
d: 9 November 1885

21 Susannah Haynes
b: 17 July 1795   cont 5
d: 17 July 1874

22 Martin Vineyard
b: 15 January 1798
d: 15 March 1853

23 Mary Louisa Jane Nance
b: 1802
d: 15 July 1847

2 Walter Ed Bell
b: 25 April 1886
p: Tennessee, USA
m:
p:
d: 3 November 1944
p: Oklahoma, USA

10 Moses A. Skeen Jr.
b: 30 April 1832
p: Jefferson, Tennessee, USA
m: 14 December 1852
p: Grainger, Tennessee, USA
d: 29 September 1906
p: Lamasco, Fannin, Texas, USA

11 Mary Jane Vineyard
b: 13 June 1831
p: Grainger, Tennessee, USA
d: 11 February 1905
p: Lamasco, Fannin, Texas, USA

5 Dorthula Jan Skeen
b: 10 October 1857
p:
d: 25 March 1947
p: Bokchito, Bryan, Oklahoma, USA

24
b:
d:

25
b:
d:

26
b:
d:

27
b:
d:

1 Floy Mae Bell
b: 5 December 1915
p: Bokchito, Bryan, Oklahoma, USA
m: 27 December 1935
p:
d: 3 May 2014
p: Big Rapids, Michigan, USA

sp: **Otho Miller Story Jr.**

12
b:
p:
m:
p:
d:
p:

13
b:
p:
d:
p:

6 Jesse Preston Meek
b: 16 October 1844
p: Bible Grove, Clay, Illinois, USA
m: 1865
p:
d: 15 September 1905
p: Lamasco, Fannin, Texas, USA

28
b:
d:

29
b:
d:

30
b:
d:

31
b:
d:

3 Mattie Meek
b: 1889
p: Oklahoma, USA
d: 21 February 1956
p: Oklahoma, USA

7 Mary Minerva Craig
b: 1848
p: Henry, Kentucky, USA
d: 20 February 1914
p: Okay, Wagoner, Oklahoma, USA

14
b:
p:
m:
p:
d:
p:

15
b:
p:
d:
p:

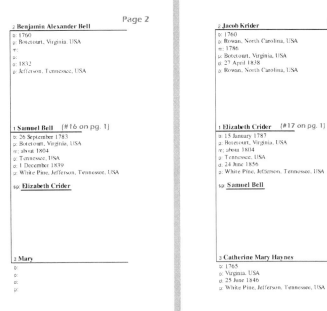

2 Benjamin Alexander Bell

b: 1760
p: Botetourt, Virginia, USA
m:
p:
d: 1832
p: Jefferson, Tennessee, USA

1 Samuel Bell (#16 on pg. 1)

b: 26 September 1783
p: Botetourt, Virginia, USA
m: about 1804
p: Tennessee, USA
d: 1 December 1839
p: White Pine, Jefferson, Tennessee, USA

sp: **Elizabeth Crider**

3 Mary

b:
p:
d:
p:

2 Jacob Krider

b: 1760
p: Rowan, North Carolina, USA
m: 1786
p: Botetourt, Virginia, USA
d: 27 April 1838
p: Rowan, North Carolina, USA

1 Elizabeth Crider (#17 on pg. 1)

b: 15 January 1787
p: Botetourt, Virginia, USA
m: about 1804
p: Tennessee, USA
d: 24 June 1856
p: White Pine, Jefferson, Tennessee, USA

sp: **Samuel Bell**

3 Catherine Mary Haynes

b: 1765
p: Virginia, USA
d: 25 June 1846
p: White Pine, Jefferson, Tennessee, USA

Continued Pedigree - Floy Mae Bell

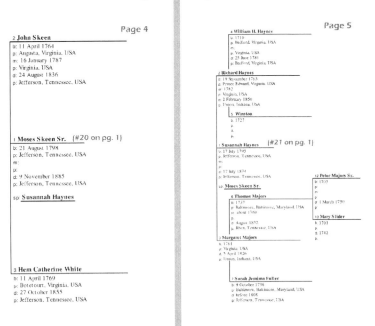

2 John Skeen

b: 11 April 1764
p: Augusta, Virginia, USA
m: 16 January 1787
p: Virginia, USA
d: 24 August 1836
p: Jefferson, Tennessee, USA

1 Moses Skeen Sr. (#20 on pg. 1)

b: 21 August 1798
p: Jefferson, Tennessee, USA
m:
p:
d: 9 November 1885
p: Jefferson, Tennessee, USA

sp: **Susannah Haynes**

3 Hem Catherine White

b: 11 April 1769
p: Botetourt, Virginia, USA
d: 27 October 1855
p: Jefferson, Tennessee, USA

4 William H. Haynes
b: 1710
p: Bedford, Virginia, USA
m:
p: Virginia, USA
d: 25 June 1781
p: Bedford, Virginia, USA

2 Richard Haynes
b: 19 September 1763
p: Prince Edward, Virginia, USA
m: 1782
p: Virginia, USA
d: 2 February 1850
p: Union, Indiana, USA

5 Winston
b: 1727
p:
d:
p:

1 Susannah Haynes (#21 on pg. 1)
b: 17 July 1795
p: Jefferson, Tennessee, USA
m:
p:
d: 17 July 1874
p: Jefferson, Tennessee, USA

sp: **Moses Skeen Sr.**

6 Thomas Majors
b: 1737
p: Baltimore, Baltimore, Maryland, USA
m: about 1760
p:
d: August 1832
p: Rhea, Tennessee, USA

3 Margaret Majors
b: 1764
p: Virginia, USA
d: 5 April 1826
p: Union, Indiana, USA

12 Peter Majors Sr.
b: 1703
p:
m:
p:
d: 1 March 1750
p:

12 Mary Slider
b: 1703
p:
d: 1742
p:

7 Sarah Jemima Fuller
b: 9 October 1736
p: Baltimore, Baltimore, Maryland, USA
d: before 1805
p: Jefferson, Tennessee, USA

CITATIONS

I Family-Tree-Maker, Cherokee Genealogy

II Documented under "William the Carpenter" Wikipedia, the Free Encyclopedia, update Oct. 2014

III Documented "Battle of Tours", Wikipedia, the Free Encyclopedia.

IV Native American Indian and Melungeons History, Genealogy, Thomas Pasmere Carpenter.

V www.theeastindiancompany.com

VI Most of the Cherokee genealogy information was found at: "Family-Tree-Maker, Cherokee Genealogy"

VII Amatoya Moytoy I (1649-1700) Genealogy, managed by Vinson Anderson, updated July 12, 2011

VIII My Southern Family, Chief Amatoya Moytoy of Chota.

IX The James Scrolls, An Indian Trail From Amatoya Moytoy to my Mother, March 26, 2009

X www.myheritage.com/person.MoytoyII, Trader Tom Carpenter

XI www.myheritage.com/person, Moytoy II, Trader Tom Carpenter.

XII www.geni.com/people/White-Owl-Raven-Moytoy-Carpenter-IV/
327599333890005354

XIII Genealogy.com/ Brown Family Roots-Information about White
Owl Raven.

XIV Family-Tree-Maker, Cherokee Genealogy

XV Family-Tree-Maker, Genealogy Site, User Home Page/ Cherokee
Lineages/ Alexander Drumgoole, Sr.

XVI Canasatego, en.wikipedia.org/wiki/Canasatego

XVII "Iroquois and the Founding Fathers
(http://www.teachinghistory.org/history-content/ask-a-historian24099)

XVIII Wikipedia http://en.wikipedia.org/wiki/Great_Law_of_Peace

XIX Family-Tree-Maker/personal, Alexander Drumgoole Sr.

XX Tennessee history, preservation and educational artifacts,
Tennessee History Classroom.

XXI Tennessee history, preservation, and education artifacts,
Tennessee History Classroom, Attakullakulla

XXII John Ehle, Trail of Tears, The Rise and Fall of the Cherokee
Nation.

XXIII Family-Tree-Maker/ Cherokee Genealogy

XXIV http://thejamesscrolls.blogspot.com/2009/chief-kanagatooga-old-hop

XXV Education & Resources - National Women's History Museum

XXVI Wikipedia.org/wiki/Cherokee, Wikipedia.org/wiki/Treaty_of_New_Echota

XXVII Cherokeeheritiage.org/female-seminaries, Cherokee Heritage Center

XXVIII Cherokee Rose, An Oklahoma Legend as retold by S. E. Schlosser

XXIX http://enwikipedia.org/wiki/Major_Ridge

XXX www.geni.com/people/Major-Ridge/6000000001637194329

XXXI History of the Boydstun Family, Major Ridge and John Ridge

XXXII Ledgend of the Cherokee Rose, from Oklahoma folklore at Americanfolklore.net

XXXIII U. S. Department of State, Office of the Historian, Indian Treaties and the Removal Act of 1830.

XXXIV http://en.wikipedia.org/wiki?Moravian_Church

XXXV Bob Blankenship, Cherokee Roots Volume II

XXXVI http://en.wikipedia.org/wiki/Stand_Watie

XXXVII http://civilwarhome.com/watiebio.htm, Shotgun's Home of the American Civil War

XXXVIII http://www.georgiaencyclopedia.org/articles/history-archaeology/cherokee

XXXIX http://wikipedia.org/wiki/Nimrod_Jerret_Smith

XL Family-Tree-Maker, Cherokee Genealogy

XLI Ancestry.com/Story-Family-and-Bell-Family

XLII Cherokee History Course, compiled by Chadwick "Corntassel" Smith

XLIII http://en.wikipedia.org/wiki/Cherokee

XLIV http://courtneymilleraughor.wordpress.com/category/cherokee-wild-potato

XLV Cherokee History Course, compiled by Chadwick "Corntassel" Smith

XLVI Myths and Legends, Journey of the Cherokees, 2007, Cherokee History Course

XLVII Traditional Religious Beliefs of the Cherokee, Cherokee History Course, 2007

49899983R00068

Made in the USA
Charleston, SC
07 December 2015